This Book Belongs To:

_____

_____

THE Dancer's
BOOK OF
Ballet Crafts

Dancewear, Accessories,
and Keepsakes

CHRISTINA ALETA HASKIN · PHOTOGRAPHS BY ROSALIE O'CONNOR

The Dancer's Book of Ballet Crafts

SENIOR EDITOR Carol Endler Sterbenz
PHOTO EDITOR Robyn Poplasky
EDITORIAL ASSISTANTS Jennifer Calvert and Nora Grace
INDEXER Schroeder Indexing Services
PRINCIPAL PHOTOGRAPHY Rosalie O'Connor
INSTRUCTIONAL PHOTOGRAPHY Steven Mays
LIGHTING DESIGNER David Cunningham
PRODUCER OF PHOTOGRAPHY Genevieve A. Sterbenz
TECHNICAL EDITOR Amy O'Neill Houck
TECHNICAL ARTIST Marta Curry
DESIGNER Goodesign

Creative Homeowner

VICE PRESIDENT AND PUBLISHER Timothy O. Bakke
PRODUCTION DIRECTOR Kimberly H. Vivas
ART DIRECTOR David Geer
MANAGING EDITOR Fran J. Donegan

Current Printing (last digit)
10 9 8 7 6 5 4 3 2 1
iPod® is a registered trademark of Apple Computers, Inc.
Lycra® is a registered trademark of the Dupont Corporation.

Photo Rights:
On page 8, Anna Pavlova, PhotoFest
On page 156, Swan Lake, Corps de Ballet, RetnaCelebs/Retna Ltd.
On page 158, Swan Lake, Pas de Deux, Fernando Aceves/Retna, Ltd.
On page 160, Sleeping Beauty, Lilac Fairy, Fernando Aceves/Retna Ltd.

Selected Quotes: www.dance.com/tom-parsons/quotes.html
On page 12, John Martin
Every effort has been made to correctly attribute quotes;
inadvertent omissions will be noted in the next printing.

The Dancer's Book of Ballet Crafts, First Edition
Library of Congress Control Number: 2006939478
ISBN-10: 1-58011-353-2
ISBN-13: 978-1-58011-353-3

CREATIVE HOMEOWNER®
A Division of Federal Marketing Corp.
24 Park Way
Upper Saddle River, NJ 07458

Dedicated to my father for giving me the gift of the love of ballet;
to my mother for her love of art and beauty; and to my daughter for
taking this inheritance one step further.

CONTENTS

$\mathcal{I}$NTRODUCTION

I have been involved in both dance and design throughout my life. My father was a ballet dancer for Ballet Theatre and, in his retirement, a ballet instructor. My mother danced throughout Europe in a sister team. Because of them, I grew up immersed in the music of Chopin and Tchaikovsky—attending ballet classes every week, steadily pouring grace into my developing muscles, and acquiring a life-long passion for moving to beautiful music. All the long hours of practice would ultimately lead to the blissful reward of appearing on stage in a recital, dressed in a sparkling costume, bathed in glorious light, and capturing the attention of an audience. I would perform my part and feel transported to another world. This world of ballet imbued me with a love of the magic of performance. To this day, the enchanting blend of art and physical exertion continues to enrich my life, as it does my daughter's whose elegant, long leg reaches across the *barre*, creating a fresh and exciting beauty for this familiar art form.

The dancer's life, rich with artistry, color, decoration, technique, practice, and self-expression has much in common with a crafts person in her pursuit of beauty and excellence. In *The Dancer's Book of Ballet Crafts*, I wanted to blend the artistry of the world of ballet and crafts into one. Ballet is an art that requires creativity and imaginative expression. No two dancers are the same. Ballet demands dedication, discipline, focus, continual practice, and technique. In the end, something beautiful emerges that brings joy to the beholder. Crafts, like ballet, require artistry, technique, concentration, imagination, and a dream of making something of beauty. In this book, I bring the worlds of ballet and crafts together, and offer 35 projects to capture the imagination and provide creative occupation for the time spent waiting outside the studio door, downtown at rehearsals, or in-between classes. Inspired by ballet's unique style, each project can be lovingly crafted as a gift or by dancers themselves. The warmth of a ballet wrap handcrafted by someone dear to her can reassure a dancer. A handmade photo album holding performance photos can become an heirloom, to be discovered by the next generation who, like every dancer before, becomes inspired to pursue the joys of ballet and crafts.

✢

Christina Aleta Hashin

THE *H*ISTORY OF *B*ALLET

Anna Pavlova in The Sleeping Beauty

The beauty of ballet has been a source of joy for people throughout the centuries. In the Italian courts, dance joined painting, poetry, and music as entertainment for the aristocracy. The Italian queen Catherine de Medici brought ballet to France when she traveled there to marry the French king. The height of court ballets (*ballet de cour*) occurred during the reign of Louis XIV, who was himself a young dancer. He danced the role of Apollo in a gold costume that resembled the sun, and thus came to be called "The Sun King." King Louis established a professional academy of dance called "The Academy of Royal Dance" in 1661. Balletic movements were then named in French, which has remained the language of ballet throughout the world.

Early dancers wore heavy wigs, elaborate headdresses, and long, cumbersome costumes. Costumes evolved to become simpler and lighter through the innovations of dancers who wanted to move more freely. Marie Taglioni, a famous Italian ballerina of the Romantic era, popularized the shortening of the skirt and dancing on the toes by virtue of her graceful and effortless movement. These innovations resulted in the tutu and pointe shoes.

Ballet today is a reflection of the time periods that most greatly influenced it throughout its evolution. The French Jean George Noverre furthered the development of the dramatic ballet (*ballet d'action*) with his famous "Letters on The Dancing of the Ballet" in 1758. In the Romantic era of the early 19th century, ballet adopted the themes that were simultaneously developing in literature and poetry. Choreographers borrowed movements from the folk culture of the day and incorporated them into ballets such as "Giselle" in 1841. As dancers traveled to foreign stages, ballet spread across Europe and to Russia. During the Classical period, French choreographer Marius Petipa entertained the czars of Russia—with the help of assistant Lev Ivanov—when the Imperial Ballet performed such pieces as Tchaikovsky's *The Sleeping Beauty*, *Swan Lake*, and *The Nutcracker*. Petipa brought the *pas de deux* into his ballets.

Mikhail Fokine, sometimes called the father of modern ballet, steered ballet from spectacle to dramatic story telling. He developed famous dancers of the period such as Anna Pavlova, Vaslav Nijinsky, Tamara Karsavina, and Mathilde Kschessinska. Forming the Ballet Russe with Serge Diaghilev, the Russians created a sensation in Paris in 1911, and revived the world's interest in ballet. After the Russian Revolution, Russian dancers immigrated to America, stimulating interest in ballet there. A Russian, George Balanchine, became one of America's great choreographers. Other choreographers, such as Anthony Tudor, Frederick Ashton, Jerome Robbins, Agnes De Mille, and Kenneth McMillian, further developed the ballet stories in a more modern form. Today, the new edge in ballet is Contemporary Ballet, where themed ballets incorporate classic technique in a more relaxed and less formal style. ✣

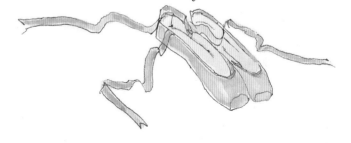

CHAPTER

BEGINNING DREAMS

The seed of a dream may be planted the moment you see the beauty of a trained ballet dancer and imagine yourself in that role, illuminated by the glow of stage lights as you take your bow of gratitude. It may be a secret dream, but the sparkle in your eyes will reveal it as you imagine pink satin and tulle, *pointe* shoes that wait to be filled, and makeup in small jars that stand ready to magically transform your eager face. As you learn to express your inner beauty, one step at a time, the desire that begins in your heart may grow into a passion for dance that helps you reach those moments of triumph, joy, and accomplishment—well-earned rewards for your heartfelt investment. As you train to become a ballet dancer, you are enticed further by beautiful costumes and sparkling tiaras, and by dancing the role of a mystical character surrounded by majestic scenery. Ballet is, after all, filled with captivating tales of magic and fairies, princes, and princesses. Most enchanting of all is crossing a threshold from everyday life to the mesmerizing world of make-believe and playing a role in an irresistible adventure. This journey transforms you from dreamer to dancer. ✣

"Let us read and let us dance, two amusements that will never do any harm to the world."

VOLTAIRE

"*The dance exists exclusively in terms of the movement of the body, not only in the obvious sense that the dancer moves, but also in the less apparent sense that its response in the spectator is likewise a matter of body movement.*"

JOHN MARTIN

ballet russe

THE BALLET RUSSE, CREATED BY RUSSIAN IMPRESARIO SERGE DIAGILIEV BROUGHT RUSSIAN BALLET TO PARIS IN 1911 WITH GREAT SUCCESS. IN SUBSEQUENT INTERNATIONAL TOURS, BALLET RUSSE REVITALIZED THE WORLD'S INTEREST IN BALLET.

MATERIALS

Tote bag, sturdy cotton, chocolate brown, 11" (27.9cm) wide and 11" (27.9cm) high

Access to a computer, scanner, and ink-jet printer

1 piece of ink-jet photo transfer fabric with adhesive backing

Scissors

Art: "Plié"
(See illustration at right.)

2 yds. (1.8m) satin ribbon, pink, 3/8" (9mm) wide

15–20 rhinestones, flat back, pink, 2.2mm (or size SS-7)

Fabric glue

Tweezers

"Plié"

A ballet bag travels everywhere with a dancer—to class, to rehearsal, and to performance spaces. An essential part of a dancer's life, the bag must be durable and compact to hold everything that is vital to a dancer. Here, a bag in chocolate brown is embellished with an original drawing that is framed in pink satin ribbons and rhinestones. Personalizing a bag is easy. All you need is access to a computer, a scanner, and transfer fabric. In moments, an ordinary bag can be turned into something unique and all your own.

DESIGNED BY CHRISTINA ALETA HASKIN AND GENEVIEVE A. STERBENZ

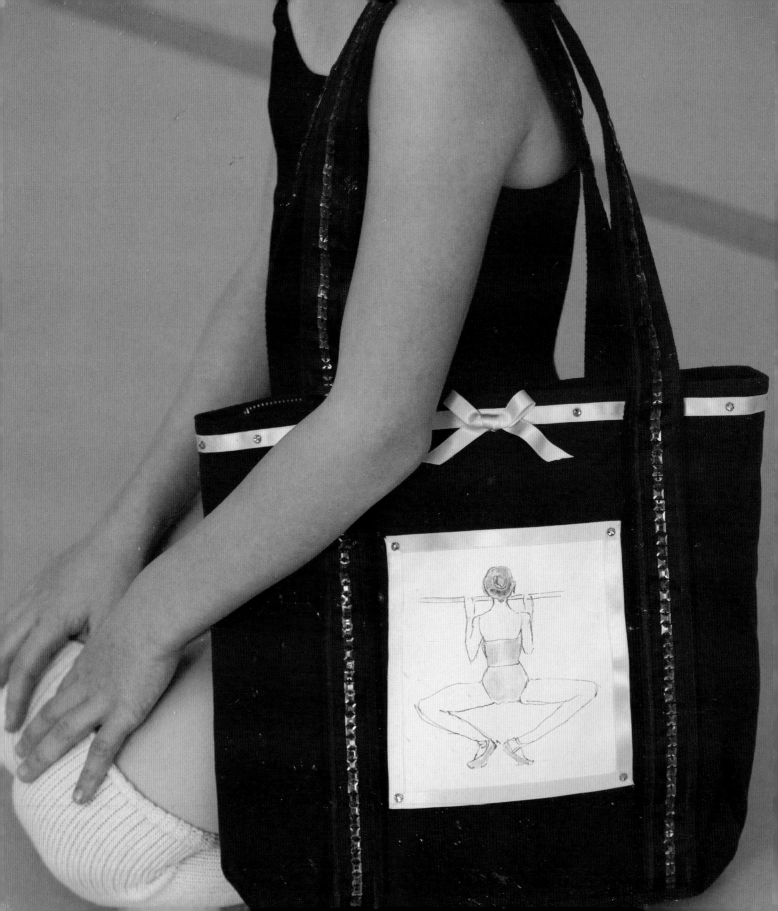

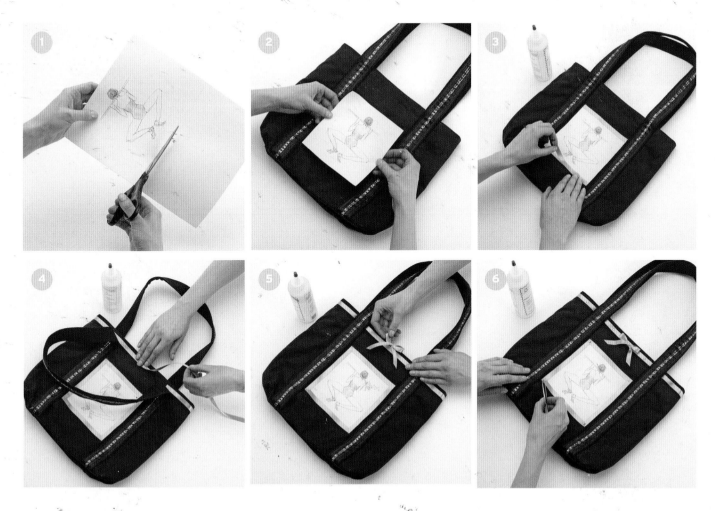

making "ballet russe"

1 Scan the illustration "Plié," on page 13, to your computer. Using photo-editing software, enlarge the image so it fits on a 5-in.-by-6-in. (12.7cm by 15.2cm) piece of fabric with 1 in. (2.5cm) of white space on all sides. Follow the instructions on the packaging for the photo transfer fabric to print your image. Use scissors to cut a 5-in.-by-6-in. (12.7cm by 15.2cm) rectangle from the fabric, making certain to center the printed image.

2 Peel away the paper backing from the transfer fabric to reveal the adhesive surface. Position and press the printed fabric onto the bag, image side facing up.

3 Measure and cut four lengths of ribbon, two for the top and bottom of the transfer fabric, and two for the sides. Cut the ends at a 45-deg. angle so the ribbon ends abut. Apply a bead of glue to the ribbon, and fix each piece to the bag, covering the raw edge of the photo transfer fabric.

4 Measure, cut, and glue a length of ribbon around the top edge of your bag, overlapping the ends in an unobtrusive place, such as behind a strap.

5 Use another piece of ribbon to tie a 3-in.-wide (7.6cm) bow. Position and glue the bow to the center of the ribbon border on the bag.

6 Use tweezers to pick up one rhinestone. Apply a dab of glue to the back of the gem, and press it, glue side down, to one corner of the ribbon frame. Continue to decorate each of the remaining corners. Apply rhinestones evenly across the band of ribbon at the top edge of the bag. Let the glue dry.

"A child sings before it speaks, dances almost before it walks. Music is in our hearts from the beginning."

PAMELA BROWN

coppélia

LOVE IS THE CENTRAL THEME IN THE BALLET *COPPÉLIA*, A STORY OF
A YOUNG PEASANT GIRL WHO PRETENDS TO BE A DOLL TO WIN BACK THE HEART
OF HER FIANCÉ. AN ENDEARINGLY SENTIMENTAL AND COMIC BALLET, *COPPÉLIA*
WAS CHOREOGRAPHED BY ARTHUR SAINT-LÉON, AND WAS FIRST PERFORMED
IN 1870 AT THE PARIS OPERA.

MATERIALS

Patterns: "Heart Purse" (A) and
"Stitching and Beading" (B)
(*See page 21.*)

½ yd. (45.7cm) satin polyester
fabric, pink

Scrap of cotton batting,
12" (30.5cm) square

Polyester thread, pink
and dark pink

Dress zipper, pink, 5" (12.7cm)
long

Sequin appliqué in heart shape,
1" (2.54cm) wide

1 vial of seed beads, cherry
pink

Permanent jewelry glue

Pkg. of fusible webbing

Large scrap of cotton fabric

Sewing machine

Household iron

Beading needle, fabric pencil,
ruler, scissors, straight pins

Bobby pins are forever "disappearing," and they become as precious as gold when, in the rush to get your hair ready before class or a performance, they elude you completely or lay hopelessly under the paraphernalia that fills your ballet bag. This pretty pink-satin purse is the perfect solution to bobby-pin organization. Made from a pale-pink satiny fabric, the purse is accented with a beaded-heart appliqué covered in seed beads in a delicious cherry-pink color. Its shape is echoed in single beads that surround it like a halo. Although the purse takes some sewing experience to make, it is well worth the effort. You will never have to look for your precious bobby pins again.

making "coppélia"

1 Photocopy and print the heart patterns (A) and (B) on page 21. Cut out pattern (A) along the cutting line, and cut out pattern (B) a scant ⅛ in. (3mm) outside of the dashed line. Use pattern (A) to cut four hearts from the pink satin fabric.

2 Lay the satin hearts flat, wrong sides up. Center and pin the heart pattern (B) on one satin heart, and trace around the perimeter of the pattern. Repeat to mark three more satin hearts as before.

3 Lay and pin two satin hearts together, right sides facing and all raw edges even. Use light-pink thread to machine-stitch around the marked line, beginning at one "X," going down to the heart's bottom point, and ending at the second "X." Repeat to sew the second set of hearts (for the lining), this time sewing a scant ⅛ in. (3mm) within the stitch line.

4 Use the scissors to snip into the seam allowance around the curves at the top of one sewn heart without cutting into the stitch line. Repeat with the second heart lining.

5 Position and pin pattern (B) to the cotton batting. Cut around the pattern to make one heart. Repeat to make a second batting heart. Use pattern (B) to cut out two hearts from the fusible webbing.

6 Lay the large scrap of fabric flat on your work surface. Lay the fusible-webbing heart on the cotton-batting heart, with all edges even. Use a hot iron to fuse the webbing to the batting heart following the directions on the packaging.

making "coppélia" continued...

7 Peel off the protective paper from the fusible-webbing heart to reveal the fusible webbing.

8 Position one batting/webbing heart on the wrong side of the smaller pair of sewn hearts (lining), matching the heart to the marked shape. Repeat to adhere the second batting/webbing heart to the other side of the heart.

9 Turn the satin heart without batting right side out. Insert the heart lining inside, smoothing the fabrics flat.

10 Fold the raw edges of both the lining and the purse exterior in toward the batting, and use a threaded needle to whip-stitch the heart lining to the heart purse around the curved sections at the top of the heart. Position, pin, and sew the zipper to the top opening of the purse, following the instructions on the packaging.

11 Lay the heart appliqué on a protected work surface. Apply a coat of glue to the center of the heart, smoothing the glue until the heart-shaped area is covered. Open the vial of beads, and sprinkle beads directly onto the glued area. Use your finger to pat down the beads; let the glue dry completely. Gently tap off any loose beads. Referring to the "Stitching and Beading" pattern, mark the position of the center heart appliqué and the individual beads.

12 Thread a needle with one strand of dark-pink thread, and make a single knot in one end. Referring to "Stitching and Beading" (opposite) sew on the beads, ending the thread with a few tiny stitches at the inside lining.

(A)

cutting line

Heart Purse

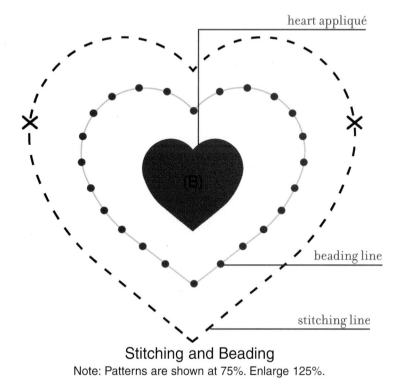

heart appliqué

(B)

beading line

stitching line

Stitching and Beading
Note: Patterns are shown at 75%. Enlarge 125%.

"*Dance first. Think later. It's the natural order.*"

SAMUEL BECKETT

jewels

THE FAMOUS CHOREOGRAPHER GEORGE BALANCHINE CREATED A THEMED BALLET
ABOUT RUBIES AND EMERALDS CALLED *JEWELS*, HIS ONLY FULL-LENGTH BALLET THAT DIDN'T
HAVE A TRADITIONAL PLOT. IT IS SAID THAT HE WAS INSPIRED BY THE STUNNING JEWELS
IN A JEWELER'S WINDOW ON FIFTH AVENUE IN NEW YORK CITY.

MATERIALS

To make one crystal-and-pearl "Jewels" bobby pin.

Plain bobby pin, 2"
(5.0cm) long, metal,
silver tone

Spool of beading wire,
32 gauge, silver tone

Wire cutters

Ruler or measuring
tape

8 cube-shaped crystal
beads, 3mm, in colors
as desired

2 freshwater pearls,
3mm

SPECIAL NOTE

You can make many other
decorated bobby pins of
your own design. See page
24 for more ideas. Then
follow the directions on
page 25, using the beads of
your choice.

*Before beginning her first class,
a young dancer has to look the
part. This includes making sure
her hair is neat, not just for style
reasons, but for the purpose of
keeping loose wisps of hair from
distracting her as she dances.
"Jewels" is the perfect hair accessory, combining beauty and
function. Making "Jewels" is an
enormously fun and simple
endeavor. A row of crystal beads
and freshwater pearls is wired to
a plain bobby pin. Make several
of your own designs; it will make
pinning up your hair more fun.*

DESIGNED BY CHRISTINA ALETA HASKIN
AND GENEVIEVE A. STERBENZ

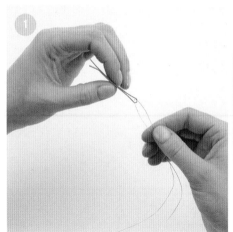

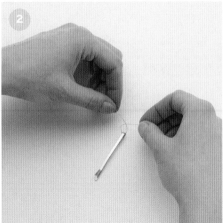

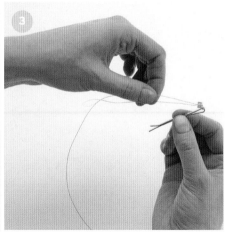

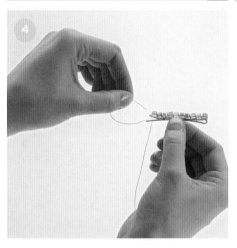

making "jewels"

1 Measure and cut a 3-ft. (91.4cm) length of wire from the spool, using the wire cutters. Thread one end of the wire through the end loop in the bobby pin. Pull the wire through until the center of the wire is at the end loop of the bobby pin.

2 Lay the pin on your work surface. Bring both ends of wire to the top of the bobby pin, and cross them. Then twist the wires once, thus creating a knot, to secure the wires to the pin.

3 Lay the crystals and pearls on your work surface in an order that pleases you, beginning the pattern with one crystal. Insert both ends of wire through one crystal, sliding it down the wire until it lays flat against the top bar of the bobby pin. Separate the wires, and cross them under the top bar, bringing them back up to the top of the bar. Wrap only one wire around the bar, and bring it back up to the top. Twist the wires once.

4 Continue to add the crystals and pearls to the bar of the bobby pin as in step 3. When all the crystals and pearls are wired, wrap both ends of the wire around the end of the bar once, and insert the ends back through the first two beads. Pull the wires taut, and snip off the extra wire.

*"To touch, to move, to
inspire, is the
true gift of dance."*

UNKNOWN

rose

THE ROSE IS A VERY POPULAR MOTIF IN BALLET COSTUMING. IT IS FOUND EVERYWHERE—
ON RIBBON TRIMS, BODICES, AND HAIRPIECES. IT IS EVEN A FEATURED CHARACTER
IN THE BALLET, *SPECTRE DE LA ROSE*. THE IDENTIFICATION OF A ROSE WITH BEAUTY,
PERHAPS, IS THE REASON FOR ITS POPULARITY IN BALLET.

MATERIALS

Hair comb, 2" (5.0cm)
long, metal, silver tone

6 artificial rose buds on
wire stems, each bud ¾"
(1.9cm) wide

3 pearl-cluster beads,
½" (1.2cm)*

*Note: These beads are clusters of
small pearls glued into a hollow
bead shape. You can use any
pearl-type bead you like of
similar size.*

*The "Rose" hair comb resembles
a small garden of pink flowers
accented with pearl clusters.
Pretty as it is practical, this elegant accessory is the perfect way
to add neat style to your hair. It
will also bring out the natural
loveliness of your face, comple-
menting the blush of rosy cheeks
that comes from joyously moving
about. The secret to making
the decorated comb is the stem
wire on each rose, which can be
easily wrapped around the comb
to secure it. "Rose" will brighten
any dance class.*

DESIGNED BY CHRISTINA ALETA HASKIN
AND GENEVIEVE A. STERBENZ

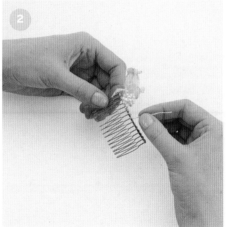

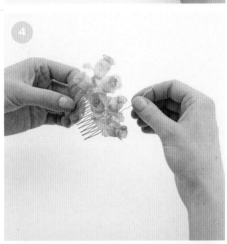

making "rose"

1 Slide one pearl-cluster bead onto each of three rosebud stems. Set two rose-and-pearl decorations aside.

2 Beginning at one end of the comb, hold the head of one rose-and-pearl decoration against the top bar of the comb with one hand, and wind the stem wire tightly around the bar and between the teeth of the comb with the other. When the rose is secure, snip off any excess stem wire.

3 Hold the head of a plain rose (without a pearl cluster), against the rose-and-pearl decoration secured in step 2. Wind the stem around the bar and between the teeth of the comb. Moving in small increments, add one rose-and-pearl and one plain rose decoration to the comb as before.

4 Add the remaining plain rose, then position the final rose-and-pearl decoration at the end of the comb, winding the stem wire around the bar in the direction of the center of the bar. Trim off the excess wire. Bend the rose heads in a pleasing array.

> *"Imagination is more important than knowledge."*
>
> ALBERT EINSTEIN

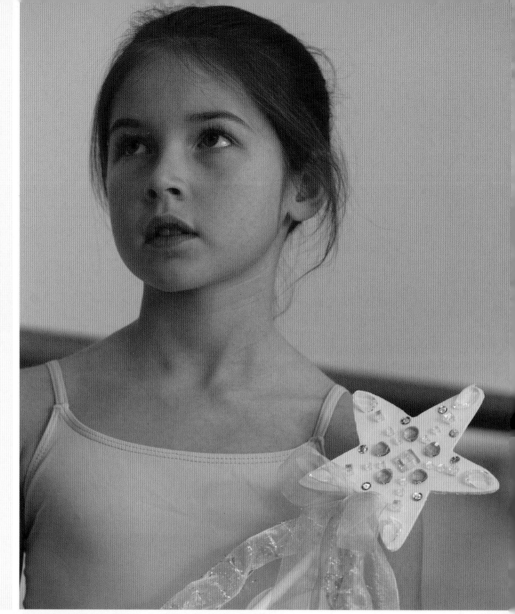

snow queen

THE SNOW QUEEN IS A CHARACTER FROM THE FAIRY TALE BY THE SAME NAME,
A RICH FANTASY WRITTEN BY HANS CHRISTIAN ANDERSEN IN 1845. LIVING IN A FROZEN WORLD,
THE SNOW QUEEN IS SAID TO TRAVEL ON THE SNOW AND RULE OVER THE SNOWFLAKES, WHICH
LOOK LIKE "BEES" AS THEY FALL TO EARTH.

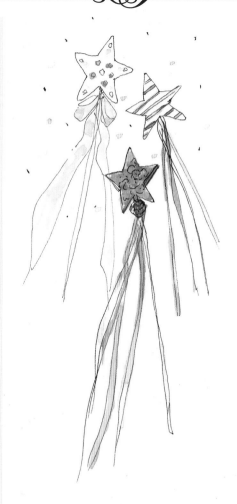

MATERIALS

Wooden star, 5" (12.7cm) wide

Wooden dowel, ¼" (6mm)
dia., cut to 24" (60.9cm) long

White acrylic paint

Sponge brush, 1" (2.5cm) wide

Crystal rhinestones, flat backs:
5 clear teardrops, ¾"
(1.9cm) dia.

5 ice blue teardrops, ⅜"
(9mm) dia.

5 clear rhinestone cubes,
¼" (6mm)

10 clear rhinestone cubes,
⅛" (3mm)

1 clear rhinestone square,
½" (1.2cm) wide

Silver sequins

Permanent jewelry glue

Hot-glue gun and glue sticks

1 yd. (.91m) metallic
ribbon, 1½" (3.8cm) wide

1 yd. (.91m) sheer ribbon,
1½" (3.8cm) wide

In many of the story ballets, wands come into play. Always magical by nature, wands let us drift into an imaginary world of dreams where spells can be cast and wishes fulfilled. Wands are great fun to make and to twirl around, especially when you are thinking of making some magic of your own. Here, our wand symbolizes the icy world of the Snow Queen, where palaces and gardens always lay under a blanket of snow. The blue and water-clear crystals that decorate the star glisten like icicles, and have an enticing quality. This wand might bring on a cold north wind, or turn a handful of stones into diamonds. All you need to begin your adventure is a wooden star, a dowel, and some decorations, and you can create a wand that takes you to any place you can imagine.

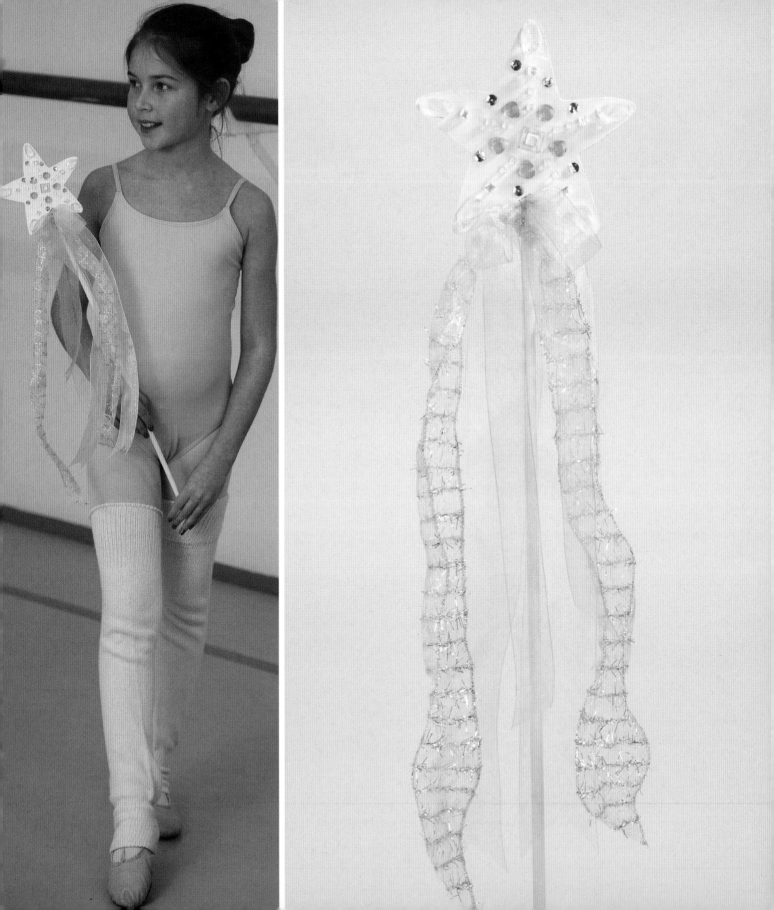

making "snow queen"

1 Lay the star on a protected work surface. Apply a thin coat of white paint to one side using the sponge brush; let the paint dry. Turn the star over, and paint the other side and the edges of the star; let it dry. Paint the dowel stick; let it dry. Apply a second coat to the star and the dowel; let the paint dry completely.

2 Lay the painted star flat. Referring to the photo on page 32, arrange the rhinestones on a flat surface. Apply a dab of glue to the flat back of the square rhinestone then position and press it to the center of the star. Continue gluing on rhinestones. Let the glue dry completely.

3 Lay the bejeweled star, wrong side up, on your work surface. Apply a 3-in. (7.6cm) line of hot glue along one end of the dowel stick, and immediately press the dowel onto the star, as shown.

4 Use the sheer ribbon to tie a ribbon bow on the dowel, allowing the streamers to cascade freely. Repeat to tie a ribbon bow using the metallic ribbon.

Variations:

There are many ways to decorate your wand. Use your imagination to design your own wand using the steps described. Be inspired by a ballet such as *Spectre de la Rose*, by Michel Fokine. In this ballet a girl dreams that the rose she holds in her hand turns into the man of her dreams, or by *The Nutcracker* ballet, in which the Sugar Plum fairy uses her magical wand to summon a parade of sweets that entertain Marie and the Prince. Below are design variations. First make the wand, following steps 1–2, then follow the suggestions described at right.

"Spectre de la Rose" uses the rose motif. To make this design, glue on single petals cut from an artificial rose to both sides of the star. Wrap the star in a piece of sheer pink organdy. Tie ribbon streamers in pink and rose colors to the dowel, adding a large rose as shown.

"Candy Cane"
This wand is inspired by the stripes on the candy canes seen in *The Nutcracker*. To make this design, glue parallel lengths of slender satin ribbons in pastel colors to the front and back of the star. Tie ribbon streamers in pink, blue, and green to the dowel.

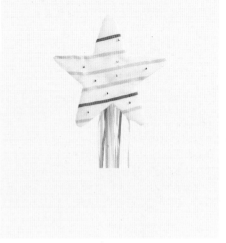

"As a profession, dance has its hazards like any other art. Nevertheless, I believe it to be the best and most agreeable life, because people who perform on the stage enjoy some sort of special magic not really found anywhere else."

MARGOT FONTEYN

étoile

THE PRINCIPAL DANCERS IN THE FAMOUS PARIS OPERA BALLET ARE CALLED *LES ÉTOILES*,
A FRENCH WORD MEANING "THE STARS." BEGUN IN 1661, THE PARIS OPERA BALLET
WAS CREATED BY KING LOUIS XIV, WHO ALSO CREATED THE ROYAL ACADEMY OF DANCE THAT REMAINS
TODAY ONE OF THE OLDEST DANCE SCHOOLS IN THE WORLD.

MATERIALS

Crystal beads:

    2 faceted clear ron delles, pink, 3mm long, 4mm dia.

    2 clear tear drops, pale pink

    2 faceted barrel shape, pale pink

Charm of ballet dancer, gold tone, or as desired

Memory wire, bright silver, bracelet weight

Jump ring, 6mm

Wire cutters

2 pairs of chain-nose pliers

Emery cloth

It is fitting that this delicate and simple bracelet be named "Étoile" because it symbolizes a dancer's dream of, one day, becoming a star. While the path to becoming a principal dancer takes a lot of hard work and time, this little bracelet is easy to make in a short time. Made of faceted crystal beads in a subtle range of color—water-clear pink, pale ballet pink, and blushing rose, the bracelet is accented by a gold charm of a ballet dancer. The charm can become a kind of touchstone of luck in your ascent to realizing your dream. Make a bracelet for yourself, and wear it after class or when you attend a ballet performance.

DESIGNED BY GENEVIEVE A. STERBENZ

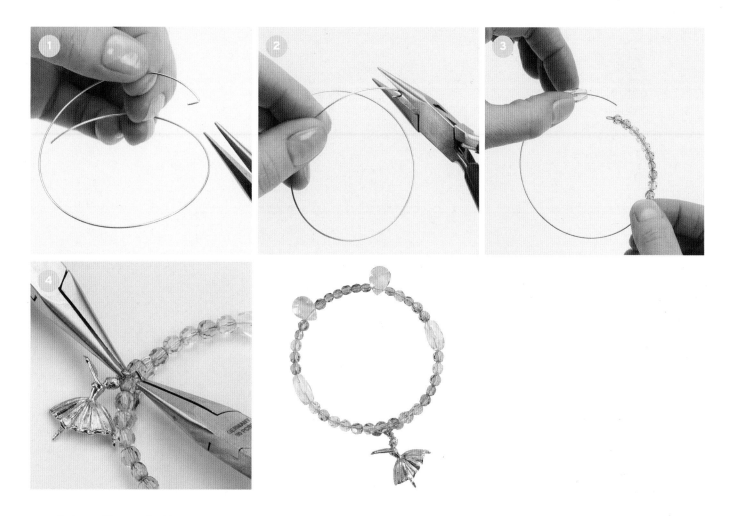

making "étoile"

1 Count one complete loop of memory wire, and use the wire cutters to cut the loop from the coil. Use emery cloth to smooth the cut ends. Use the tips of the chain-nose pliers to bend the wire ⅛ in. (3mm) from one end.

2 Use a wider section of the pliers' jaws to squeeze the end flat to the wire.

3 Thread the opposite end of the wire through eight rondelles and one barrel-shaped bead. Slide the beads along the wire until they reach the bent end. Continue to add beads in the following order: five rondelles, one tear drop, six rondelles, one tear drop, five rondelles, one barrel-shaped bead, and the remaining eight rondelles.

4 Use the chain-nose pliers to bend the end of the memory wire and squeeze the end flat as in steps 1–2. Use both sets of pliers to open the jump ring. Thread one end of the jump ring through the hanging loop on the charm and around the wire, between the last two beads on the bracelet. Close the jump ring.

CHAPTER

2

WARMING UP

Everyday cares, frustrations, and concerns are slowly set aside as student dancers make their way to the ballet studio in time to warm up before class. They enter the studio, rushing past the wall posters of famous dancers whose brilliant artistry continues to inspire them. Then, a sense of quiet settles in as their focus shifts inward to a place of peaceful concentration where they connect with the ideals of beauty and perfection that they aspire to express in their dance. As they change out of their everyday clothes, pulling knitted leg warmers over their graceful limbs, the students begin to stretch and flex their muscles in a familiar routine that they have performed countless times before. Dancers know that it is essential to warm up so that their muscles and joints are flexible enough for the more complex movements of class. In a crowded hallway, legs extend this way and that. Each dancer's warm-up is tailored to his or her needs, focusing on muscle groups and feet, all in an effort to limber up and prepare the body and spirit for the demands that lie ahead. ✧

"To dance is to be out of yourself. Larger, more beautiful, more powerful. This is power, it is glory on earth and it is yours for the taking."

AGNES DE MILLE

*"Only the
wise
can dance
the rhythm
of life."*

UNKNOWN

pas de chat

THE PAS DE CHAT MOVEMENT IS SO NAMED BECAUSE IT RESEMBLES THE
GRACEFUL LEAP OF A CAT. THE FEET ARE LIFTED, ONE AFTER THE OTHER,
TO THE LEVEL OF THE OPPOSITE KNEE.

SKILL LEVEL
Beginner

FINISHED SIZE
Circumference: 12"
(30.5cm) at ankle
Length: 13" (33.0cm)

YARN
The Australian Yarn
Company, "Breeze": 30%
wool, 69.6% cotton, 0.4%
Lycra; [98 yds. (90m)/1.7
oz. (50g)]

CA: coral, color #0112, 1 ball

CB: red, color #018, 1 ball

CC: yellow, color #003, 1 ball

CD: turquoise, color #011, 1 ball

CE: black, color #017, 1 ball

NEEDLES
1 pair size 7 (4.5mm)
double-pointed

1 pair size 9 (5.5mm)
double-pointed

GUAGE
20 sts and 30 rows = 4"
(10.1cm) in st st

(continued on page 43)

Knitted in the folk-art style, these
striped ankle warmers have a
vitality of color and an energy all
their own. The vibrant colors
"bounce" as though encouraging
the dancer to leap to stardom. A
shorter "cousin" of the leg warmer,
the ankle warmer insulates the
warmth produced by stretching the
muscles. The knitted fabric hugs
and protects the ankles, which are
particularly vulnerable to injury.
Slowly stretching the foot and
ankle invigorates the body's natural elasticity, and allows for a
more fluid performance.

DESIGNED BY TINA RAE DEAN

making "pas de chat"

(continued from page 41)

SPECIAL STITCHES
The leg warmers are worked in the round, two consecutive rows per color in the order listed in the "Yarn" list. Yarns not being used can be carried up the inside of the work.

ABBREVIATIONS
See page 174.

FIRST ANKLE WARMER
BOTTOM RIBBING
With CA, cast on 63 stitches (21 stitches per needle) using size 7 needles (4.5mm). Join to work in the round. Work k1, p1 rib, changing color every 2 rows according to order in yarn list, until rib measures 1½" (3.8cm) from cast-on edge.

LEG
Change to Size 9 (5.5mm) needles. Knit each row, continuing color changes every two rows until work measures 12" (30.5cm) from cast-on edge.

TOP RIBBING
Work in k1, p1 rib with next color in pat for 3 rows. Work remaining colors 2 rows each in k1, p1 pattern until work measures approximately 14" (35.6cm) from cast-on edge. Change to CA and bind off in k1, p1 pattern. Weave in ends.

SECOND ANKLE WARMER
Repeat to make second ankle warmer.

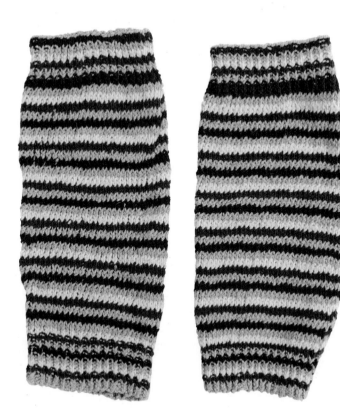

> *"Dancing with the feet is one thing,*
> *but dancing with the heart is another."*
> —UNKNOWN

cameo

A CAMEO ROLE IS ONE PLAYED BY A FAMOUS DANCER WHO MAKES A
BRIEF BUT CHERISHED APPEARANCE IN A BALLET. YOUNG CHILDREN IN AN
IMPORTANT PRODUCTION CAN ALSO DANCE CAMEO ROLES.

SKILL LEVEL
Beginner

FINISHED SIZE
Circumference: 10"
(25.4cm) at ankle
Length: 16" (40.6cm)

"Cameo" is for a younger
dancer. The seam is on the
inside of leg with pattern
centered on the outside.

YARN
Berroco Pure Merino: 100%
extra fine merino wool;
[92 yds. (85m)/ 1.7oz.(50g)]

MC: color #8512 "Bellarina."
3 balls, approx. 234 yds. (214m)

CC: a few yards in contrasting
color #8500, "Snow Bunny"

NEEDLES
1 pair size 9 (5.5mm)

NOTIONS
Stitch markers
Yarn needle

GUAGE
14 sts and 19 rows = 4" (10.1cm)
in st st

(continued on page 47)

Single white hearts play cameo
roles in these adorable knitted leg
warmers. The knitted hearts sym-
bolize the singular and dedicated
love of ballet that a dancer experiences in the beginning stages of
study, and that prevails throughout the years of long practice—for
dancing requires heart. When this
love of ballet is expressed in a
dancer's performance, the audience always receives a special gift.
Knitting from the heart is also a
joyful experience. Knit these practical and pretty leg warmers; they
are easy to make, either for yourself or for a gift.

DESIGNED BY JEANNIE FINLAY

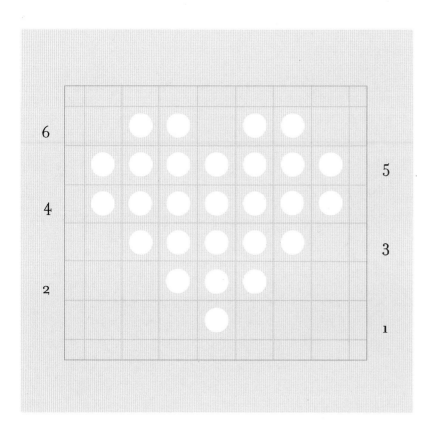

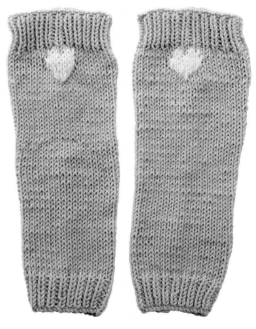

making "cameo"

(continued from page 45)

SPECIAL STITCHES

M1 = make one stitch: with left needle, pick up running yarn between stitches from front to back, knit through the back, creating one new twisted stitch.

ABBREVIATIONS

See page 174.

FIRST LEG WARMER

BOTTOM RIBBING:

With MC, cast on 34 stitches.

Row 1: *(k1, p1) rep from * to end for row. Continue ribbing for 2" (5cm).

Leg:

Row 1: (RS) K17, pm, k17.

Row 2: P.

Row 3: (increase row): K1, m1, k32, m1, k1 (36 sts).

Row 4: P.

Row 5: K.

Continue in st st. Rep row 3 (increase row) every 12th row until work measures 14" (35.6cm) from cast-on edge. End on WS row.

BEGIN HEART PATTERN:

Row 1: K1, m1, k to marker. Join CC and k1, with MC, k19, m1, k1.

Row 2: With MC, p20, with CC, p3, with MC, k to end.

Row 3: With MC, k20, with CC, k5, with MC, k to end.

Row 4: With MC, p18, with CC, p7, with MC, p to end.

Row 5: With MC, k19, with CC, k7, with MC, k to end.

Row 6: With MC, p19, with CC, p2, with MC, p1, with CC, p2, with MC, p to end.

Row 7: With MC, k .

Row 8: With MC, p.

TOP RIBBING:

Work in k1, p1 rib for 2" (5cm), and bind off ribbing.

FINISHING:

With right sides facing and side edges touching, sew up back seam using blanket stitch. Weave in ends.

SECOND LEG WARMER

Repeat to make second leg warmer.

*"Dance is the movement of the universe
concentrated in the individual."*

ISADORA DUNCAN

danilova

ALEXANDRA DANILOVA WAS A RUSSIAN-BORN PRIMA BALLERINA *ABSOLUTA*.
SHE IMMIGRATED TO AMERICA WITH GEORGE BALANCHINE TO ESCAPE
THE RUSSIAN REVOLUTION. SHE WAS A DANCE PARTNER TO BALANCHINE,
AND ONE OF THE MOST PROMINENT BALLET STARS OF HER ERA.

SKILL LEVEL
Beginner

FINISHED SIZE
Circumference: 8" (20.3cm)
at ankle

Cuff hugs foot and thigh, and
ankle features opening for heel
Length: 26" (66cm)

YARN
Cascade, "Bollicine Baby Night":
100% extra fine merino wool;
[95 yds. (87m)/1.7oz.(50g)]

MC: 4 balls

CC: (white, #1) 1 ball [approx.
40 yds (36.6m)]

NEEDLES
1 pair size 6 (4mm) straight

2 pairs size 6 (4mm) circular:

9" (22.9cm) and 16" (40.6cm)
long (*or size needed to obtain gauge*).

NOTIONS
Stitch markers

Yarn needle

GUAGE
20 stitches and 28 rows = 4"
(10.1cm) in st st

(*continued on page 51*)

Warming up for class and enduring long rehearsals in cold theatres is much easier when these tubes of softly-knitted fabric are slipped over the calves and knees. A dancer's staple, leg warmers insulate a dancer's legs and ankles, conserve the warmth that will protect them from injury, and allow a dancer to be her best. The "Danilova" leg warmers feature a black field of knitted fabric that frames a line of pretty white intarsia hearts. Making your own leg warmers will allow you to add touches of personal style to your warm-up routine.

DESIGNED BY JEANNIE FINLAY

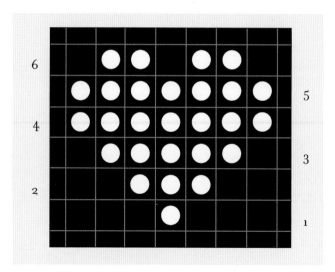

making "danilova"

(continued from page 49)

SPECIAL STITCHES

M1 = make 1 stitch: with left needle, pick up running yarn between stitches from front to back, knit through the back, creating one new twisted stitch.

ABBREVIATIONS

See page 174.

LEFT LEGWARMER

RIBBING: With MC, cast on 42 stitches with straight needles.

Row 1: (RS) Join second strand of MC, work k1, p1 with yarn doubled for 2" (5cm). End on WS row. Break off one strand of yarn.

LEG:

Row 1: (RS) sl, k 40, sl.

Row 2: P.

Repeat Row 1 and Row 2 for 4" (10cm). End on WS row.

BEGIN HEART PATTERN:

Row 1: Knit stitches onto 9" (22.8cm) circular needle, pm, join to work in round, pm at beg of round.

Round 2: With MC, k7. Place different colored marker to denote beg of heart chart, k7, place different colored marker to denote end of heart chart, k around.

Round 3: K1, m1, k to 1st chart marker, sm, with MC, k3, with CC, k1, with MC, k3, sm, k to 1 bef end of rnd, m1, k1.

Round 4: K to 1st chart marker, sm, with MC, k2, with CC, k3, with MC, k2, sm, k around.

Round 5: Knit to 1st chart marker, sm, with MC, k1, with CC, k5, with MC, k1, sm, k around.

Round 6-7: Knit to 1st chart marker, sm, with CC, k7, sm, k around.

Round 8: Knit to 1st chart marker, sm, with MC, k1, with CC, k2, with MC, k1, with CC, k2, with MC, k1, sm, k around. (end chart, slip chart markers as you go but continue to work in MC until heart begins again)

Round 9: K1, m1, k to 1 st bef end of rnd, m1, k1.

Round 10-17: K.

Round 18: Rep row 9.

Repeat complete pat: rounds 3–18, remembering to k1, m1 at each end every round 3 and round 9 until you have 70 stitches. At this point, you may want to transfer work onto 16" (40.6cm) circular needle. Continue repeating pat, this time also increasing 1 stitch on each end in round 7, round 10, round 14, and round 18 until you have 94 stitches or 19" (42.3cm) around for thigh. Work even in pat until leg measures 24" (61cm) from joined seam at top of heel.

Join second strand of MC yarn and k2, p2 with yarn doubled for 2" (5cm) more [26" (66cm) from seam at top of heel]. Bind off, and weave in ends. Sew bottom ribbing at side edges.

RIGHT LEG WARMER

Begin as left leg with 42 stitches and follow until "Begin Heart Pattern."

Row 1: Knit stitches onto 9" (22.8cm) circular needle, pm, to mark beg/end of rnd, join to work in round.

Round 2: With MC, k 28, place different colored marker to denote end of heart chart, k around. Work rounds 3–18, finishing as for left leg.

CHAPTER

3

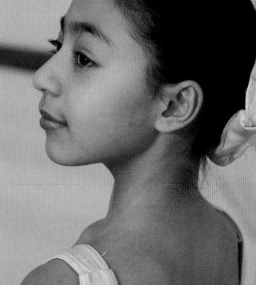

At the Barre

After dancers complete their preliminary warm-up, they stream into the studio and find their places at the *barre*. They move together through a series of exercises that develops their strength and skill, and that prepares them for their work in the *centre*. At the sound of the first note of music from the piano, dancers gently wrap their hands around the smooth wooden barre, descending into the first *plié*. Continuing in a sequence of movements, legs turn out, toes point, and extensions rise higher and higher. All the while, an encouraging ballet teacher observes them, correcting their posture and adjusting the positions of their feet and hands to help the dancers achieve a more elegant line. When barre exercises are performed not only with technical precision but with passion and vitality, dancers get used to dancing more freely and with heart. The practice of moving with expression at the barre is a prelude to moving with confidence during a performance when the pressure for perfection is high. Dancers work hard at the barre, knowing their technique will serve them well in calming jittery nerves and allowing them to surrender to the unity of motion and music that elevates dance to poetic ballet. ✝

"Dance for yourself. If someone else understands, good.
If not, then no matter, go right on doing what you love."

LOUIS HORST

53

"I explained it when I danced it."

MARGOT FONTEYN

snowflake

FOR THE MUSIC OF "THE WALTZ OF THE SNOWFLAKES" IN *THE NUTCRACKER* BALLET, TCHAIKOVSKY INCLUDED THE USE OF A CHILDREN'S CHORUS.

SKILL LEVEL
Experienced

FINISHED SIZE
3.5" (8.9cm) across top of bun warmer

HOOK
Hook: F/5 (3.75mm)

YARN
J&P Coats Royale Silkessence Microfiber: 100% acrylic microfiber; [124 yds. (113.4m)/2 oz. (56.7g)], white

NOTIONS
Approximately 40 class "E" seed beads

Hair elastic

Beading needle

Tapestry needle

GUAGE SWATCH
Work Rnds 1–4 of pattern; swatch should measure 3" (7.6cm) in dia.

(continued on page 57)

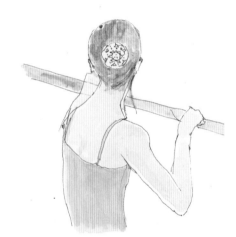

Young ballerinas have often been labeled "bun heads" because of the famous hairstyle often used in ballet practice classes. This bun cover (or snood) is a traditional way to keep hair in place. The snowflake design, crocheted with small beads, is pretty and practical. The beads are worked into the stitch as you crochet so that they are securely attached to the bun cover. Once you learn to add beads to your crochet fabric, you can create variations on this bun-cover design for your classes and performances.

DESIGNED BY DEE STANZIANO

STITCH KEY

- • Slip Stitch = Sl
- ◠ Chain = Ch
- ■ Beaded Chain = Bch
- + Single Crochet = Sc
- ✛ Beaded Single Crochet = Bsc
- T Half Double Crochet = Hdc
- ⍕ Double Crochet Cluster = Cl
- ⍏ Double Crochet Decrease = Dc dec
- ⲻ Beaded Triple Crochet = Btr

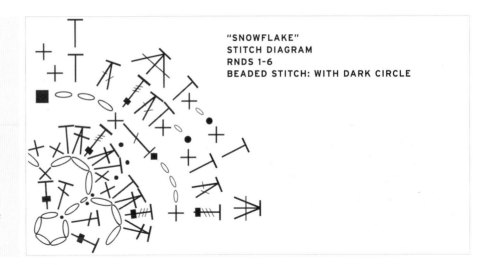

"SNOWFLAKE"
STITCH DIAGRAM
RNDS 1-6
BEADED STITCH: WITH DARK CIRCLE

making "snowflake"

(continued from page 55)

SPECIAL STITCHES

Bch: (beaded chain) Slide bead next to hook, yo and draw yarn through loop on hook

Bsc: (beaded single crochet) Insert hook into st, yo draw up loop, slide bead next to hook, yo and draw yarn through loops on hook.

Btr: (beaded treble crochet) Yo twice, insert hook into st, slide bead next to hook, yo and draw yarn though 2 loops, yo draw through 2 loops, yo again and draw through last remaining loops.

CL: (cluster) Yo, insert hook in st and draw up loop, yo draw through two loops, yo, insert hook into next st, yo and draw up loop, yo draw through two loops, yo and draw through last three loops.

Dc dec: (decrease) Yo, insert hook into st, draw up loop, yo, draw through two loops, yo insert hook into next st and draw up loop, yo and draw through two loops, insert hook into next st and draw up loop, yo and draw through two loops, yo again and draw through all loops on hook.

Ch-sp: Chain sp, the chains between stitches where new stitches are often worked in the following row or round.

BEADS

Pre-string beads onto crochet thread. *Note: all beads will show on back side of the work. When done, invert the "Snowflake" bun cover to show the beads.*

BUN COVER

Ch 6, sl st into 1st chain to form a ring.

Rnd 1: Ch 1, (sc,bsc), 8 times into center of ring, join rnd with sl st. (16 sts)

Rnd 2: Ch, 1 bsc in same st as sl st, ch 3, sk 1 st, *bsc in next st, ch 3 sk 1 st, repeat from * around, join with sl st. (8 sts, 8 ch-sps)

Rnd 3: Ch 1, (sc, hdc, CL, btr, CL, hdc, sc,) in each ch-dp around. Join rnd with sl st. (8 "petals")

Rnd 4: Sl st in hdc, CL and in btr *ch 3, bch, ch3 sl st to next btr, repeat from * 6 more times, ch 3 bch, dc into last btr completing the round. (8 loops)

Rnd 5: Ch 1, * working over dc st and to the left of bch created in Rnd 4, (sc, hdc, CL,), btr. in next st, working over ch-sp and to the right of the bch, (sc hdc, CL) repeat from * around join with sl st. *Note: Beads from Rnd 4 should be showing.*

Rnd 6: Ch 1, sc in same st, hdc in next, dc dec, hdc, sc, *sc, hdc, dc dec, hdc, sc, repeat from * around, join with sl st.

Rnd 7: Ch 2, hdc around, join with sl st. *Note: To create a smaller bun cover for thinner, shorter hair, omit this rnd. To accommodate thicker, longer hair, Rnd 7 may also be repeated as needed to increase the size of "Snowflake" bun cover.*

Rnd 8: Ch 1, hold elastic next to work, sc over elastic and into each st around, join with sl st. Finish off.

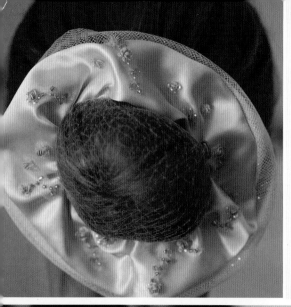

" Dance is the hidden language of the soul. "

MARTHA GRAHAM

sleeping beauty

IN *SLEEPING BEAUTY*, AURORA DANCES THE "ROSE ADAGIO" WITH FOUR SUITORS
AT HER 16TH BIRTHDAY. EACH PRESENTS HER WITH A ROSE, AND SHE BALANCES IN ATTITUDE
AS EACH OF THE SUITORS PROMENADES HER.

MATERIALS

1¼ yds. (1.1m) pink satin
ribbon, double faced,
3" (7.6cm) wide

¼ yd. (22.8cm) white tulle

Approx 1 yd. (91.4cm) ribbon
with sequined roses, ⅝"
(15mm)* wide

½ yd. (45.7cm) elastic cording, thin

Pink thread

Hand-sewing needle

Permanent fabric adhesive

2 safety pins

Scissors

Ruler

Sewing machine

*Note: This ribbon will be taken
apart so that the sequined roses
can be appliquéd to the scrunchy.
If you don't have access to ribbon
like this, you can use another type
of bead or rhinestone for decoration.*

Before going to class, a dancer
must remove all her jewelry and
pull back her hair into a neat bun.
In these ways, she can move freely
without being distracted by jan-
gling necklaces or strands of hair.
While dancers may appear similar
to one another when they follow
these traditions, they find creative
ways to express their unique style.
One way is by wearing scrunchies,
the pretty ruched or fan-shaped
sleeves of fabric that encircle their
buns. Making a scrunchy is simple
and fun. Inspiration for a design
can come from the colors or decorative motif of one of your favorite
ballets. Here, a practice scrunchy
in classic pink satin adorned with
sweet roses and a touch of glittered
tulle is inspired by the ballet
Sleeping Beauty.

DESIGNED BY BETH VOGL

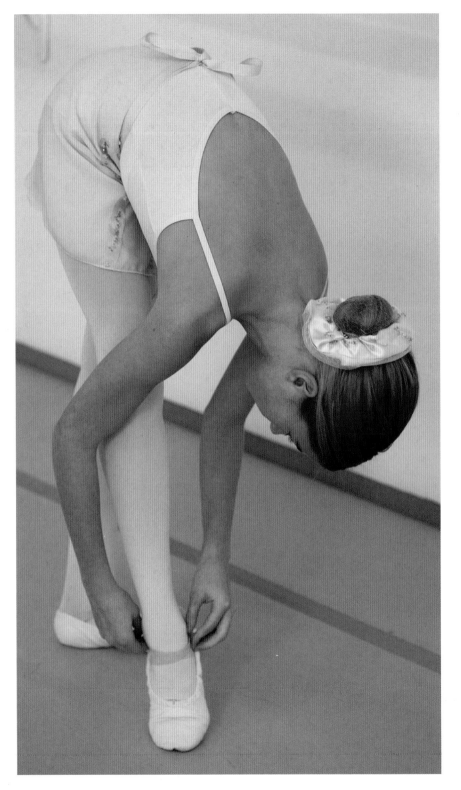

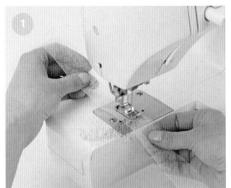

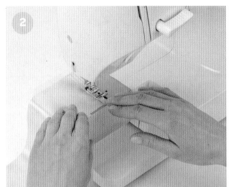

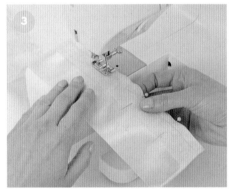

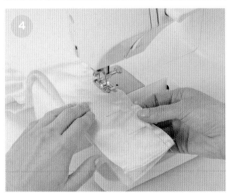

making "sleeping beauty"

1 Measure and cut a 2-in.-by-20-in. (5.0cm x 50.8cm) rectangle from the tulle fabric. Fold the tulle in half lengthwise. Machine-stitch the tulle, ⅜ in. (9.0mm) from the raw edge.

2 Measure and cut two 20-in. (50.8cm) lengths of pink satin ribbon. Fold under, and machine-stitch a ⅜-in.-wide (9.0mm) hem on each raw edge of each ribbon.

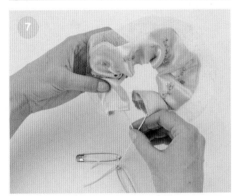

3 Lay one satin ribbon, right side up, on a flat surface. Position and pin the tulle to the ribbon, matching the raw edges of the tulle and the finished edge of the ribbon. Machine-stitch the layers together, ⅜ in. (9.0mm) from the edge.

4 Lay the second satin ribbon over the satin-and-tulle section, sandwiching the tulle between, aligning all edges, and pinning them together. Machine-stitch the ribbons along the same sewn edge ⅜ in. (9.0mm) from the edge, removing the pins as you work.

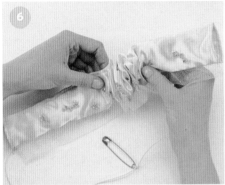

5 Open the ribbon, and lay it flat, tulle side up. Snip off sequin roses from the length of sheer ribbon. Dab the back of one sequin rose with permanent adhesive. Position and press the rose to the satin ribbon. Continue to glue roses to the satin ribbon in positions as desired, leaving 1 in. (2.5cm) at the ends of the ribbon without decoration. Fold the ribbon in half lengthwise, right sides together, and pin the edges. Machine-stitch along the full length, ⅜ in. (9.0mm) from the edge to make a tube. Turn the tube to the right side.

6 Measure and cut a length of elastic cord. *Note*: You will need 5 in.–10 in. (12.7cm–25.4cm) of elastic cord, depending on the thickness of the ponytail and number of times you want the scrunchy to wrap. Secure a safety pin to each end of the cut length of elastic. Insert one safety pin into the ribbon tube, and work it through until it exits the opposite opening.

7 Secure the ends of the elastic with a double knot. Remove the safety pins. Insert one end of the tube into the other so that ⅜ in. (9.0mm) overlaps.

8 Use a threaded needle and the whipstitch to sew the ends of the tube together.

*"Anyone who thinks
sunshine
is happiness
has never danced
in the rain."*

UNKNOWN

baby ballerina

WHEN GEORGE BALANCHINE BEGAN AS A CHOREOGRAPHER WITH THE BALLET RUSSE DE MONTE CARLO, HE CHOSE THREE TEENAGE BALLERINAS, TATIANA RIABOUCHINSKI, TAMARA TOUMANOVA, AND IRINA BARONOVA, FOR HIS NEW COMPANY. BECAUSE THEY WERE SO YOUNG, THEY WERE NICKNAMED "BABY BALLERINAS."

SKILL LEVEL: Experienced

FINISHED SIZE
Chest: 26" (66.0 cm)
Length: 15" (38.1cm)

YARN
Patons Lacette: 39% nylon, 36% acrylic, 25% mohair; [235yds. (214.9m)/1¾oz. (50g)], color #30415, Hint of Rose, 3–4 balls

NEEDLES
Size 4 (3.5mm) straight

2 size 4 (3.5mm) double-pointed

1 cable

HOOK
E/5 (3.75mm)

NOTIONS
2 decorative beads, 10mm

Stitch Markers

GUAGE
24 sts and 28 rows = 4" (10.1cm) in honeycomb pat

ABBREVIATIONS
See page 174.

Wearing a classic ballet wrap sweater has been one way for a dancer to keep warm while warming up and working at the barre. Here, a wrap sweater in the traditional style is knitted in a soft angora yarn, but instead of the typical knit-and-purl pattern usually associated with this type of sweater, a delicate honeycomb stitch pattern is used. The appeal of the wrap sweater is its adjustable fit. Knitted ties are wrapped and tied at the front of the sweater, at any tension, creating a comfortable, body-hugging silhouette. Knit this sweater for your "baby ballerina" as a loving gift.

DESIGNED BY LENA BUNEVITSKY

STITCH KEY

I	Knit
-	Purl
V	Knit, inserting the right needle into the previous row.
I - -	Sl next st to cn and hold in front, p2, then knit from cn.
- - I	Sl 2 sts to right needle, sl 1 st to cn, sl 2 sts from right needle back to left, knit from cn, p2.

STITCH CHART FOR PATTERN #1 "HONEYCOMB"

I	-	-	-		-	I	I	-	-	-	I	7
-	-	I	I	-	-	-	-	I	I	-	-	5
-	-	I	I	-	-	-	-	I	I	-	-	3
I	-	-	-		-	I	I	-	-	-	I	1

All WS rows work following the pattern (purl, when it was knitted on the RS, and knit, when it was purled on the RS side).

STITCH CHART FOR PATTERN #2

V	-	-	-	V	-	-	-	7
V	-	-	-	V	-	-	-	5
V	-	-	-	V	-	-	-	3
V	-	-	-	V	-	-	-	1

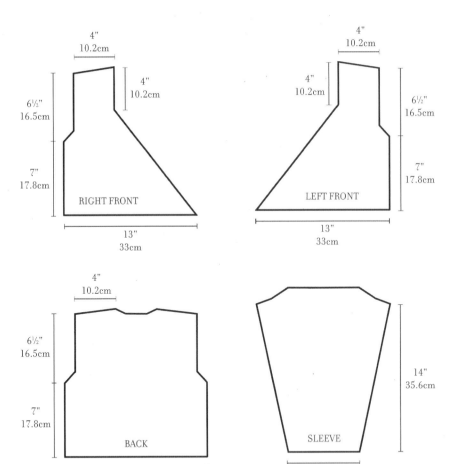

"Baby Ballerina" Diagrams

making "baby ballerina"

RIGHT FRONT

Cast on 80 sts with size 4 (3.5mm) needles

Row 1: k1 *(k1, p4, k1) rep from * to last st, p1. Begin following chart for honeycomb pat.

SHAPE WRAP FRONT AND ARMHOLES

Beg on 3rd row dec 1 st at beg of each RS row 10 times, then every 4th row 26 times, and at the same time, when front measures 7" (17.8 cm), BO 4, then 3, then 1 st at the beg of the next 3 WS rows. Continue front shaping until 36 sts rem, and front measures 10" (25.4 cm). Change the pat.

Row 1: (RS) K1, *(p2tog, p2tog) rep from * to last st, k1. (24 sts rem)

Row 2: P1 (k2, p2) to last 3 sts, k2,p1.

Row 3: K1, (yo, p2tog, yo, k2tog) to last 3 sts, p3.

Row 4: (k3, p1) across. Beg to work chart for pat #2. Continue in chart for 3.5" (8.9cm), ending with RS row.

SHAPE SHOULDER

Row 1 (WS): BO 5 sts, work in pat to end of row.

Rows 2-4: Follow the pat.

Rows 3-5: BO 6, work in pat to end of row. BO all rem sts.

LEFT FRONT

Work as for front, reversing shaping.

BACK

Cast on 86 sts with US size 4 (3.5mm) needles.

Row 1: K1 *(k1, p4, k1) rep from * to last st, p1. Beg following chart for honeycomb pat. Continue to work in pat until back measures 7" (17.8 cm).

SHAPE ARMHOLE

Row 1-2: BO 4 sts, work in pat to end of row.

Rows 3-4: BO 2 sts, work in pat to end of row.

Rows 5-6: BO 1 st, work in pat to end of row. Continue to work rem sts in pat until back matches fronts in length. (minus shoulder shaping).

SHAPE RIGHT SHOULDER

Mark the center of the back (36 sts).

Row 1: (RS) BO 5 sts, work in pat to marker. Turn, leaving rem 36 sts unworked.

Row 2: BO 4 sts, work in pat to end of row.

Row 3: BO 6 sts, work in pat to end of row.

Row 4: Work in pat to end of row.

Rows 5-6: Work as rows 3 and 4.

Row 7: BO 7 sts, work in pat to end of row. BO.

SHAPE LEFT SHOULDER

With RS facing, join yarn to rem 36 sts.

Row 1: BO 4 sts, work in pat to end of row.

Row 2: BO 5 sts, work in pat to end of row.

Row 3: BO 3 sts, work in pat to end of row.

Row 4: BO 6 sts, work in pat to end of row.

Rows 5-6: Work as rows 3 and 4.

Row 7: BO 7 sts, work in pat to end of row. BO.

SLEEVES

Cast on 32 sts.

HEM

Row 1: (RS) K.

Row 2: P.

Rows 3-8: Rep rows 1 and 2

Row 9: (WS) K1, yo, k2tog; rep from * across (Fold row for hem.)

Row 10: P.

Rows 11-16: Rep rows 1 and 2 (hem completed)

Row 17: K1, m1, k2, (m1, k3) 9 times, m1, k1, m1, k1.

Row 18: P.

Row 19: (RS) K1 *(k1, p4, k1) rep from * to end, p1.

Work in Honeycomb patt, at the same time inc 1 st at each edge every 7th row (19 times) until there are 82 sts and

sleeve measures 14" (35.6 cm) from the hem.

SHAPE CAP

Rows 1-2: BO 4 sts, work in pat to end of row.

Rows 3-4: BO 3 sts, work in pat to end of row.

Rows 5-6: BO 2 sts, work in pat to end of row.

Rows 7-10: BO 1 st, work in pat to end of row. BO rem sts.

Sew underarm seam. Fold and sew hem in place (WS).

ASSEMBLY

Sew shoulder seams, side seams, and sew in both sleeves.

CROCHETED FRONT AND NECK EDGE

With RS facing, using size E (3.75 mm) hook, start from right front work around the neck and left front. Crochet evenly: (chain st, 5 double crochet, chain st) repeat to the end of the edge.

BOTTOM EDGE

With size 4 (3.5mm) needles and RS facing, pick up evenly 140 sts. Work the hem following instructions for the sleeve. Fold and sew hem in place (WS).

TIES

Using dpns, work i-cord as follows: Make 2 ties measuring 13" (33 cm). Thread one end of each tie through a decorative bead. Make 2 more ties measuring 7" (17.8 cm).

FINISHING

Sew one long tie to right front edge and short one to left front edge.
Sew one short tie to right inner side seam just above the hem, and second long tie to left outside seam.

CHAPTER

4

IN THE CENTRE

As the piano sounds the notes of a rapturous melody of classical music, dancers move to the center of the floor—the *centre*—continuing their practice of technique and artistry through a sequence of beautiful movements. Music fills the studio, and the teacher demonstrates a set pattern of movements that the dancers follow. The sequence begins with a *port de bras*—a movement of the arms, which must be soft and expressive to be beautiful, and where the head and eyes follow the hand as it moves through the air. *Centre* work continues with an *adagio*—slow sustained movements that require balance and poise. These are followed by series of single, double, and triple *pirouettes*. As the momentum of work in the *centre* builds, the dancers move to *petit allegro*, making quick steps in increasingly intricate combinations, or *enchainements*, followed by *grande allegro*, or jumps, that are performed across the floor, causing the dancers to appear as if they are "flying." Slowly the dancers cool down, and the class ends with a *reverence*, a reverential movement, either a simple curtsy or a graceful *port de bras*, to thank the teacher for her efforts. ✚

"A day I don't dance is a day I don't live."

ANONYMOUS TUNISIAN DANCER

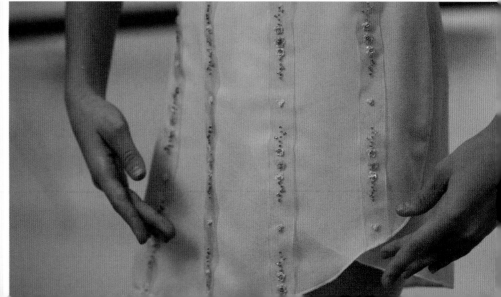

"Dance is a delicate balance between perfection and beauty."

UNKNOWN

taglioni

MARIA TAGLIONI'S FATHER, FILLIPPI, WAS HER TEACHER AND CHOREOGRAPHER.
BECAUSE HE CONSIDERED HER ARMS TOO LONG, HE DEVELOPED THE STYLE OF THE
ROUNDED ARMS TO SHORTEN THE LOOK OF THEM; IT HAS BEEN PART OF THE
ROMANTIC STYLE OF DANCE EVER SINCE.

MATERIALS

Ballet skirt, wrap style, sheer, pink

2 yds. (1.8m) pink organdy ribbon accented with beaded-ribbon roses

Matching thread

Tape measure

Straight pins

Pencil

Notepad

Newsprint paper

Hand-sewing needle

Scissors

Permanent fabric adhesive

Household iron

Dancewear for class differs from the more lavish costumes worn during a performance. For ballet class, the attire must be simple and uncluttered to allow for freedom of movement and the proper alignment of the body. The classic ballet wrap skirt is often worn as a pretty addition to a dancer's leotard. A charming alternative to the traditional skirt, our embellished skirt is created using beaded-and-sequined ribbon roses. Decorated with graceful ribbon "stripes" that are dotted with beaded roses, the skirt is transformed from day-to-day class attire to a skirt reminiscent of Parisienne-style skirts portrayed in Renoir paintings. A dab of glue and a few stitches give the dancer an understated glamour that is flowery, beautiful, and yet appropriate for class work.

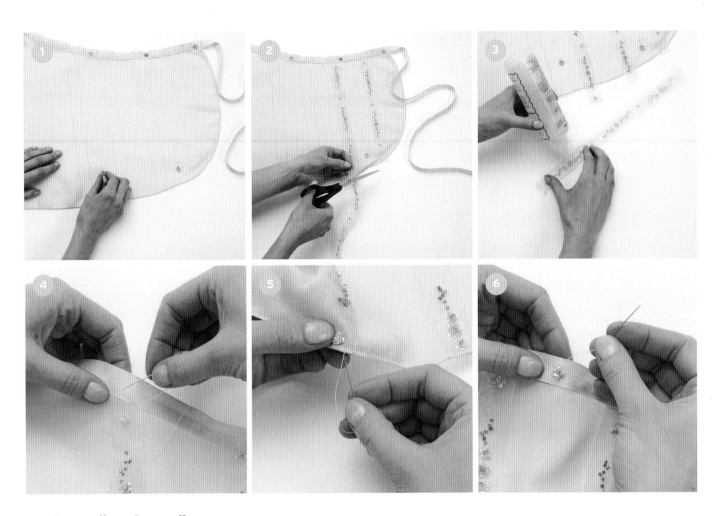

making "taglioni"

1 Trace the shape of your skirt onto the newsprint paper to make a paper pattern. Cut out the pattern, and lay it flat. Measure and mark four sets of parallel lines, 1 in. (2.5cm) apart, at 5-in. (12.7cm) intervals. Lay the skirt over the pattern as shown, using pins to secure the layers. *Note: You should see the drawn lines through the sheer skirt fabric.*

2 Measure and cut four lengths of ribbon, each ½ in. (1.2cm) longer than the drawn lines on the pattern.

3 Lay the lengths of ribbon, wrong side up, on a flat surface.

Apply a dab of adhesive to the center back of each beaded rose-and-leaf motif along one length. Position and press the length, glue side down, to the skirt using the marked lines on the pattern as a guide. Repeat to glue, position, and press the remaining ribbons to the fabric. Let the glue dry thoroughly.

4 Use a threaded needle to sew each end of ribbon at the top to the skirt, tucking the ribbon end beneath the ribbon waistband.

5 Turn under a scant ¼ in. (6.0mm) of the bottom of the ribbon at the

bottom of the skirt. Use a threaded needle to tack the ribbon to the hem.

6 Cut a few medium-size roses from the unused ribbon, trimming away the excess ribbon around the bloom. Apply a dab of glue to the back of one rose. Center and press the rose, glue side down, on the ribbon waistband, at the midpoint between each ribbon. *Note: For extra security, tack each rose in place using a threaded needle.*

Care: *It is important to gently wash the skirt by hand and then hang it up on a skirt hanger to dry. The skirt can also be dry-cleaned.*

"I see dance being used as communication between body and soul to express what is too deep to find in words."

RUTH ST. DENIS

juliet

THE BALLET ADAPTATION OF SHAKESPEARE'S *ROMEO AND JULIET* REQUIRES ACTING AND
EXPRESSIVENESS NOT SEEN IN MANY BALLETS TO CONVEY THE TRAGEDY OF THE
STAR-CROSSED LOVERS. THUS, THE MALE AND FEMALE DANCERS PLAY ROLES OF EQUAL WEIGHT
IN *ROMEO AND JULIET'S* "PAS DE DEUX," ADDING AN EMOTIONAL QUALITY TO THEIR DANCING.

SKILL LEVEL: Intermediate

SIZE(S): S (M, L)

FINISHED MEASUREMENTS
Bust: 33 (35, 37)"
[83.8 (88.9, 94)cm]

Length: 15 (15, 16)"
[38.1 (38.1, 40.6)cm]

YARN
Royal Yarn Cashsoft DK:
50% extra fine merino,
40% acrylic microfiber,
10% cashmere [142yds
(130m)/1¾oz (50g)],
color #520 7 (7, 7) balls

NEEDLES
1 pair size 5 (3.75mm)

1 size 5 (3.75mm) 32"
(81cm) circular (or size to
obtain gauge)

NOTIONS
One extra size 5 (3.75mm)
needle (for 3-needle bind off)

Yarn needle

GAUGE
24 Sts and 32 rows =
4" (10cm) in St st

*This lovely rose-colored sweater
has demure innocence. Knitted in
a delicate eyelet pattern, the tex-
ture is a subtle, yet elegant, coun-
terpoint to its otherwise simple
shape. Made in the wrap style, the
sweater is cropped to the waist,
providing freedom of movement.
Knitted in the softest pink wool,
"Juliet" is a sweater that has
timeless style and will keep you
warm while you are stretching or
simply outside on a chilly day.*

DESIGNED BY STINA RAMOS

STITCH KEY

I	Knit
-	Purl
V	Knit inserting the right needle in the previous row.
I - -	S1 next st to cn and hold infront,p2, then knt from cn.
- - I	S1 2 sts to right needle, s1 1 st to cn, s1 2sts from right needle back to left, knit from cn,p2

STITCH CHART #2

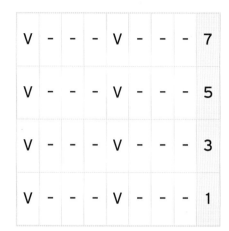

STITCHES CHART #1: HONEYCOMB

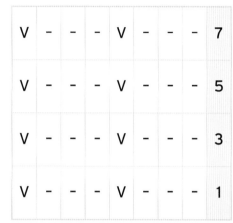

"Juliet" Diagrams

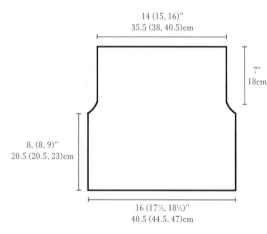

14 (15, 16)"
35.5 (38, 40.5)cm

7"
18cm

8, (8, 9)"
20.5 (20.5, 23)cm

16 (17½, 18½)"
40.5 (44.5, 47)cm

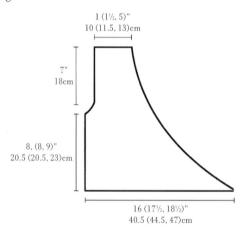

1 (1½, 5)"
10 (11.5, 13)cm

7"
18cm

8, (8, 9)"
20.5 (20.5, 23)cm

16 (17½, 18½)"
40.5 (44.5, 47)cm

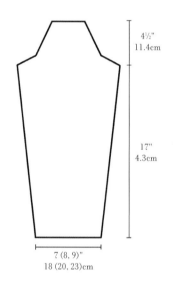

4½"
11.4cm

17"
4.3cm

7 (8, 9)"
18 (20, 23)cm

making "juliet"

BACK:
Cast on 98 (105, 112) sts.
Row 1: (WS) P.
Row 2: K.
Row 3: P.

BEGIN PATTERN:
ROW 4: (RS) (1st eyelet row) K6. *yo, k2tog, k6* rep from * to *.
Rows 5-9: Work in St st.
Row 10: (RS)(2nd eyelet row) K2 *yo,

k2tog, k6* rep from * to * end with k2.
Rows 11-15: Work in St st.
Rep rows 4–5, until piece measures 8 (8, 9)",
[20¼cm, (20¼cm, 23cm)] from CO.

SHAPE ARMHOLE:
Rows 1-2: BO 3 sts at beg of each row.
Rows 3-6: BO 2 sts beg each row.
Note: Be sure to adjust eyelet pattern so eyelets align on pat rows (rows 4 and 10).

Work even in pat until armhole measures
7" (18 cm). Leave remaining sts on a
stitch holder (for 3-needle bind off).

RIGHT FRONT
Cast on 98 (105,112) sts.
Row 1: (WS) P.
Row 2: K.
Row 3: P.

BEGIN PATTERN:

Row 4: (RS) (1st eyelet row) K6. *yo, k2tog, k6* rep from * to *.

Rows 5-9: Work in St st.

Row 10: (RS) (2nd eyelet pat, beg front edge shaping): sl 1. BO 2, k3 * yo, k2tog, k6* rep from * to * across, end with k2.

Continue to BO for wrap edge every RS row: sl 1, BO 2, 10 more times; remember to adjust pat so eyelets align on rows 4 and 10.

Rows 11-15: Work in St st.

Continue working in pat, repeating rows 11–15; after 10 more BOs, change to bind off 1st at every RS front edge until 24 (27, 30) sts rem on needle. At the same time, when front measures 7" (18.0cm).

BEGIN TO SHAPE ARMHOLE:

On 1st WS row BO 3 sts.

On 2nd and 3rd WS row, BO 2 sts.

Continue in pat with wrap edge decreases only until armhole measures 7" (18cm). Leave remaining sts on extra needles or stitch holder (for 3-needle bind off).

LEFT FRONT

Row 1: P (WS).

Row 2: K.

Row 3: P.

BEGIN PATTERN:

Row 4: (RS) (1st eyelet row) K6. *yo, k2tog, k6* rep from * to *.

Rows 5-9: Work in St st.

Row 10: (RS) (2nd eyelet pattern) K2 * yo, k2tog, k6 * rep from * to *, across, end with k2.

Row 11: (WS) (begin BO for wrap edge) Sl1, BO 2 purlwise.

Continue to BO every WS row: sl1, BO2, 10 more times. Remember to adjust pat

so eyelets align on rows 4 and 10.

Rows 11-15: Work in St st.

Continue working in pat repeating rows 11–15, after 10 more BOs, change to BO 1st at every WS /front edge until 24 (27, 30) rem on needle. At the same time, when front measure 7" (18cm).

BEGIN TO SHAPE ARMHOLE:

On 1st RS row BO 3 sts.

On 2nd and 3rd RS row, BO 2 sts.

Note: Remember to adjust pattern so eyelets align on rows 4 and 10.

Continue in pat until armhole measures 7" (18.0cm). Leave remaining sts on extra needles or stitch holder (for 3-needle bind off).

SLEEVES (MAKE TWO)

Cast on 42 (49, 56) sts.

Knit 2 rows.

Rows 3-5: Work in St st.

BEGIN PATTERN:

Row 6: (RS) (1st eyelet row) k6. *yo, k2tog, k6* rep from * to *.

Rows 7-11: Work in St st.

Row 12: (RS) (2nd eyelet pattern): K2 * yo, k2tog, k6 * rep from * to *, across, end with k2.

Row 13-17: Work in St st.

BEGIN SLEEVE INCREASES

Repeat rows 6–17 and begin increasing 1 st at each side at next RS row, then again every 5th row until you have 78 (84, 90) sts. Remember to adjust pat so eyelets align on rows 6 and 12.

Continue to work even in pat until sleeve measures 17 1/2" (44 1/2cm).

SHAPE CAP:

Rows 1-2: BO 3 sts at each edge.

Rows 3-6: BO 2 sts at each edge.

Continue to BO 1 st on each edge in every row until piece measures 5" (12 1/2cm) from the start of cap shaping and 3 1/2 (4 1/2, 5 1/2)" [9cm, (11 1/2cm, 14cm)] across and 21 (27, 33) sts.

FINISHING

Join shoulders using 3-needle BO.

Sew in the sleeves.

Sew the side and sleeve seams.

EDGING:

Using circular needle, pick up stitches evenly, starting at the back and picking up all the way around both fronts of garment. With RS facing, purl 1 row, and then bind off knit wise.

TIES (MAKE 2)

Cast on 4 sts. Knit every row until tie is 24" (60.9cm) or desired length. Remember that the tie will stretch. Attach the ties to the front lower edge of both sides. Alternate style: omit the ties and close the wrap by tying the points of the front together.

*"Freedom to a dancer
means discipline.
That is what technique
is for — liberation."*

MARTHA GRAHAM

petrushka

THE FIRST SCENE OF THE BALLET, *PETRUSHKA*, BY MICHEL FOKINE, OPENS AT A FAIR
IN SAINT PETERSBURG, RUSSIA, DURING A CARNIVAL. IN THE EXCITING
ATMOSPHERE OF A MINGLING CROWD—REPLETE WITH ORGAN GRINDER, A DANCING GIRL,
AND THREE PUPPETS—AN OLD WIZARD APPEARS. USING HIS FLUTE TO CAST
A MAGIC SPELL, THE PUPPET FIGURES COME TO LIFE—THE CLOWN-LIKE PETRUSHKA,
THE LIVELY BALLERINA DOLL, AND THE FLASHY MOOR.

MATERIALS

¼ yd. (22.8cm) double-
faced satin ribbon, non-
acetate, deep navy,
2" (5.0cm) wide

12–15 metallic stars, gold

12–15 rhinestones, silver

¼ yd. (22.8cm) elastic
cord

Matching thread

2 safety pins

Scissors

Ruler

Tweezers

Permanent glue

Household iron

Sewing machine

Hand-sewing needle

*This pretty scrunchy is created as
a tribute to the artistry, fantasy,
and resplendent scenery of
Petrushka. Made from a wide
satin ribbon in cobalt blue, the
scrunchy is fun to decorate with
silver stars and shimmering
rhinestones. Combined, they are
much like the color and sparkle of
the sky that overarches the scene
in the actual ballet. If you choose,
you may make the scrunchy in a
different color, or you may add
more decoration, such as sequins,
if you want a more festive look.*

DESIGNED BY CHRISTINA ALETA HASKIN
AND GENEVIEVE A. STERBENZ

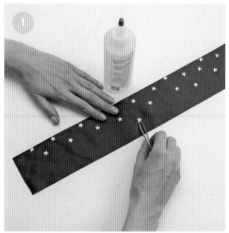
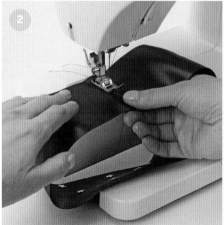
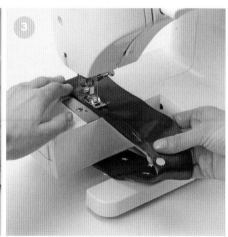

making "petrushka"

1 Measure and cut a 20-in. (50.8cm) length of ribbon, using the ruler and scissors. Lay the ribbon flat. Use tweezers to position the silver stars on the ribbon in a random pattern, adhering each with a dab of glue. Repeat to glue on the rhinestones in a random pattern. Let the glue dry. *Note: Do not place any decorations within ½ in. (1.27cm) of the raw ends of the ribbon.*

2 Fold and pin the ribbon in half lengthwise, wrong sides facing and ends even. Machine-stitch the ends

together, ¼ in. (6.0mm) from the raw edge. Fold and pin the ribbon in half, this time with right sides facing. Machine-stitch a seam, ⅜ in. (8.0mm) from the fold, trapping the raw ends of ribbon inside.

3 Fold under, iron, and pin a ½ in. (1.27cm) hem along the entire length on one side of the selvedge edge of the ribbon. Machine-stitch the hem, a scant ⅛ in. (3.0mm) from the selvage, being careful to leave an opening for the elastic cord.

4 Measure and cut the elastic cord to 8 in. (20.3cm). *Note: You will need 5in.–10in. (12.7cm–5.4cm), depending upon the number of wraps around your ponytail.* Attach a safety pin to each end of the elastic cording. Insert one into the casing, and work it through the casing until it exits the opposite opening. Remove the safety pins, and tie the cord in a double-knot. Sew the opening in the casing closed using a hand-sewing needle and the whipstitch.

ON POINTE

╬╬

Synonymous with the image of a ballerina are pink satin *pointe* shoes that elongate a dancer's legs and accentuate the magnificent lines of her feet, making her an ethereal vision as she dances on pointe. From the moment a young dancer puts on her ballet slippers, she dreams of the day when she can tie the ribbons of her first pair of pointe shoes and dance on her toes. However, it is only after years of training when a dancer's feet and legs have grown strong that her dream of dancing "on toe" will come true. The famous ballerina Marie Taglioni, of the Romantic Era, darned her ballet slippers to toughen them at the tips so that she could dance on her toes in an effort to appear weightless. Today pointe shoes have toe boxes that provide secure support for pointe work. Even in today's world of mass production, pointe shoes are shaped by cobbler's hands to make sure that they are hard enough to support a dancer but pliable enough to allow the foot to move. Each dancer has to find the make of shoe that conforms best to her foot and is suited to the type of dancing that she will perform. And when the ballerina makes her entrance on the grand stage, her grace and beauty will command the stage and her pointe work will create an illusion of being suspended in air—otherworldly and supremely elegant, a gift that will delight and uplift the audience. ✚

╬╬

"Please send me your last pair of shoes, worn out with dancing
as you mentioned in your letter,
so that I might have something to press against my heart."

JOHANN WOLFGANG VON GOETHE

"We should consider every day lost
that we have not danced at least once.
And we should call every truth false
which was not accompanied by a laugh."

JOHANN WOLFGANG VON GOETHE

parisienne

GAIETÉ PARISIENNE IS A BALLET ABOUT THE LIFE OF THE CAN-CAN DANCERS, ALSO MADE FAMOUS BY THE PAINTINGS OF TOULOUSE-LAUTREC. DANCERS ALEXANDRA DANILOVA AND FREDERICK FRANKLIN MADE A FILM VERSION WITH MUSIC BY JACQUES OFFENBACH TO PRESERVE THIS BALLET.

FINISHED SIZE

11" (29.5cm) wide

15" (37.5cm) high
incl. drawstring casing

MATERIALS

½ yd. (45.7cm) lace tulle with one scalloped border

Pink thread

Pink satin ribbon:
1 yd. (91.4cm), 1" (2.5cm) wide

1½ yds. (1.1m), ½" (1.3cm) wide

Tape measure

Scissors

Straight pins

Household iron

Safety pins

For the dancer, there is little to compare to the light and delicate feeling of being on pointe. *To the spectator, the dancer appears to be an ethereal vision on stage and presents the illusion of floating and elevation. However, contrary to its seemingly effortless appearance, dancing on* pointe *is very difficult and requires long hours of training. After many hours of use,* pointe *shoes require liberal exposure to the air so that they can dry out. Here, we have designed a lacy bag that provides a pretty and practical place to keep a pair of* pointe *shoes. The elegant French lace (that allows for air circulation) and the satin ribbons combine to make a charming drawstring bag that is a welcome change from the traditional shoe bag made of ordinary mesh fabric.*

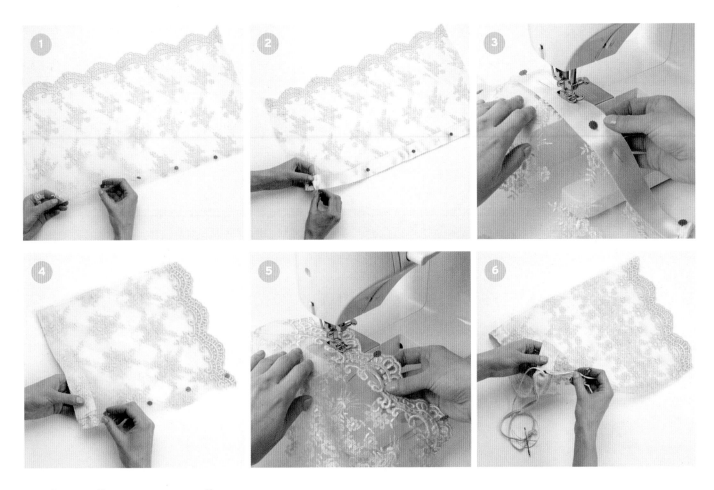

making "parisienne"

1 Measure and cut a 23-in.-wide-by-17-in.-high (58.4cm x 43.1cm) rectangle from the lace. *Note: make sure the shorter measurement uses the scalloped trim.* Lay the rectangle of lace flat, right side facing, with the scalloped side at the bottom edge. Fold over a 3/8 in. (9.0mm) hem along the top raw edge of lace, pinning the fold to secure it. Use an iron to press the fold flat. Machine-stitch the fold a scant 1/8 in. (3.0mm) from the folded edge.

2 Measure and cut one 21-in. (53.3cm) length of 1-in.-wide (2.5cm) satin ribbon for the bag casing. Fold under 1/2 in. (1.27cm) of ribbon at each end, and use an iron to press the folds flat. Center and pin the length of ribbon to the lace rectangle, lining up the edge of the ribbon with the fold of the lace.

3 Run two lines of machine stitching along the top and bottom of the ribbon, sewing it to the lace and creating a casing. *Note: the outside stitch line should be 1/8 in. (3.0mm) from the edge of the ribbon; the second line should be 1/8 in. (3.0mm) inside the first.*

4 Fold the rectangle in half, and pin side edges, right sides together. Machine-stitch along one side, 5/8 in. (16.0mm) from the raw edge, beginning at the scalloped edge at the bottom, stop-ping at the casing, and then continuing to the folded edge at the top to make a tube. *Note: Do not sew across the casing.*

5 Turn the tube right side out. Mark, pin, and sew a straight line across the bottom of the bag, 1 3/8 in. (3.5cm) above and parallel with the scalloped edge.

6 Cut a 42-in. (1.1m) length from the 1/2-in.-wide (1.2cm) ribbon to make the drawstring. Attach a safety pin to one end of the ribbon, and insert it into the opening of the casing. Thread the pin through the casing, exiting at the opposite opening. Pull the lengths of ribbon even, and sew across their raw edges.

"*Dancing is the poetry of the foot.*"

JOHN DRYDEN

cinquième

IN FRENCH, *CINQUIÈME* MEANS "FIFTH"—AN APT NAME FOR AN EMBROIDERY PROJECT THAT ILLUSTRATES THE FIFTH POSITION ON *POINTE* AND IS USED TO DECORATE A LITTLE SACHET THAT FITS INSIDE A *POINTE* SHOE TO KEEP IT FRESH AND FRAGRANT.

MATERIALS

Art: *"Pointe* Shoes" drawing (See page 88.)

Access to a photocopy machine

⅛ yd. (10.1 cm) white linen fabric

Thread: white sewing; 6-strand embroidery in dark pink

Dressmaker's tracing paper

Ruler

Pencil

Scissors

Embroidery needle

Embroidery hoop

Seam ripper

Sewing machine

Steam iron

Purchased sachet filled with cedar or lavender

Embroidery is like drawing with thread; stitch-by-stitch a picture unfolds. Here, a pair of pointe shoes is depicted in a delicate embroidery created with pink thread. The simple design includes only the essential lines, but they are enough to represent a dancer's feet posed in a closed fifth position. The classic pointe shoe motif is embroidered in a simple backstitch on fine white linen, but any outline stitch may be used to the same effect. When the embroidery is finished, the linen is paired with another piece and sewn into a small pouch into which a fragrant sachet is slipped. (The sachet can be purchased already filled with cedar or lavender buds.) Place one "Cinquième" into the box of each of your pointe shoes to keep them fresh.

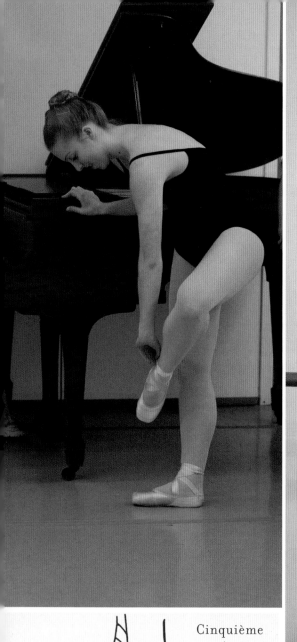

Cinquième
Art

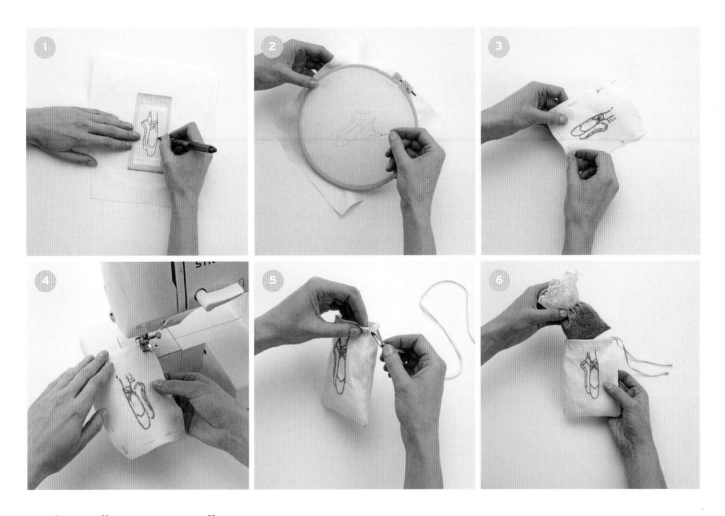

making "cinquième"

1 Use a copier or scanner to make a print of the art, "Cinquième." Measure and cut two 3⅝-in.-by-5½-in. (9.2cm by 14cm) rectangles of linen. Using dressmaker's tracing paper and a pencil, center and trace the copy of the *pointe* shoe motif onto one linen rectangle.

2 Secure the linen rectangle (with the motif) in the embroidery hoop. Thread an embroidery needle with six strands of dark pink thread, and stitch along the marked lines of the drawing using the back stitch.

3 To make the bag, position and pin the linen rectangles together, with all edges even and right sides facing. *Note: the wrong side of embroidered motif will be facing up.*

4 Machine-stitch the bag on three sides ⅜ in. (9.5mm) from the raw edge, removing the pins as you work.

5 To make the ribbon casing, turn under a ¼-in. (6.0mm) hem. Press the hem with a hot steam iron to secure the fold. Fold the top edge again, ½ in.

(1.2cm), and press it flat. Top stitch the hem a scant ⅛" (3.0mm) from the edge.

6 Turn the bag to the right side. Use a seam ripper to open the casing at the side seam. Secure a safety pin to one end of the ribbon, and insert it into the casing, working it through until it exits the opposite opening. Pull the ribbons even, and knot each end.

7 Insert a sachet of fragrant herbs into the bag, and pull the ties to close the bag. Repeat to make a second bag.

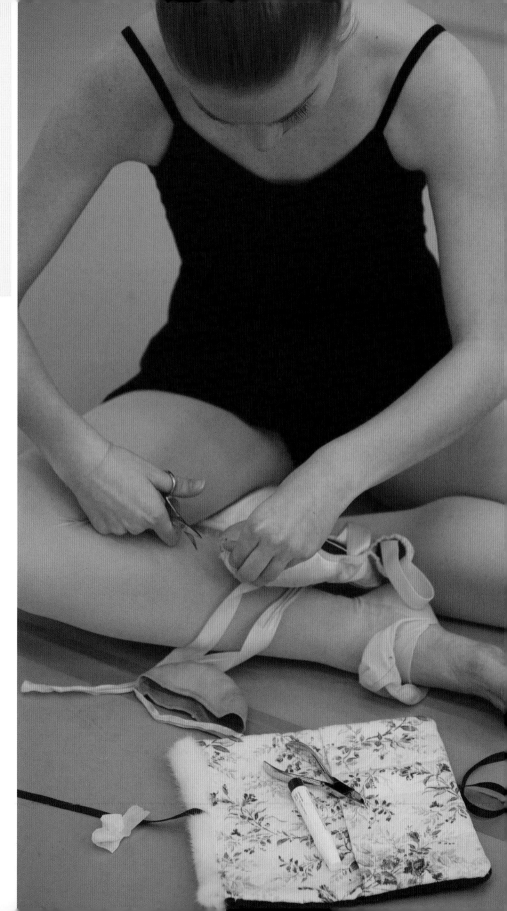

> *"The artist is nothing without the gift, but the gift is nothing without the work."*
>
> EMILE ZOLA

anastasia

ANASTASIA IS BELIEVED TO HAVE BEEN THE ONLY SURVIVOR OF HER ROYAL FAMILY'S
ASSASSINATION IN 1918 BY THE BOLSHEVIKS DURING THE RUSSIAN REVOLUTION.
BASED ON THE TRAGIC STORY OF THIS FAMOUS RUSSIAN PRINCESS, SIR KENNETH MAC MILLAN
CREATED THE MODERN BALLET *ANASTASIA*, A DRAMATIC BALLET THAT REQUIRES
GREAT ACTING ABILITY BY THE DANCERS.

MATERIALS

- ½ yd. (45.7cm) quilted velvet, cardinal red
- ½ yd. (45.7cm) quilted cotton, floral motif (for lining)
- ½ yd. (45.7cm) white cotton flannel (for interfacing)
- ½ yd. (45.7cm) white fur or faux-fur trim with ribbon binding
- ½ yd. (45.7cm) satin ribbon, ⅜" (9.5mm) wide, red
- Matching thread
- Ruler
- Dressmaker's pen, washable
- Scissors
- Household iron
- Sewing machine
- Hand-sewing needle
- Pins

Taking care of your feet after hours of dancing in pointe *shoes is essential to keep them healthy, vital, and ready to dance again. Reviving tired feet can mean a warm footbath, a foot massage, and a pedicure. This case made in quilted velvet can travel with you anywhere. When the envelope-style case is unfolded, its floral quilted lining is revealed, as are the roomy pockets that can hold all of your foot-care necessities. Its pretty satin ties and faux fur trim add touches of luxury to remind you to pamper your precious feet.*

SEWN BY PATRICIA CZESCIK

91

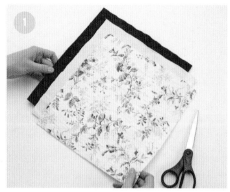

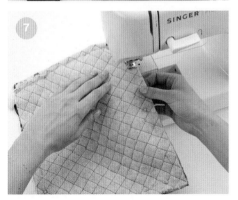

making "anastasia"

1 Measure and cut a 10-in.-by-11-in. (25.4cm by 27.9cm) rectangle from the red-quilted velvet, the floral fabric, and the flannel interfacing. Lay the floral fabric, right side up, on top of the flannel interfacing, aligning all raw edges: set the pieces aside.

2 Measure and cut a 10-in. (25.4cm) square from the floral fabric. Fold the fabric in half, and iron the fold flat. Lay the folded square flat, fold at the top edge. Measure and mark four vertical lines on the folded fabric, measuring from the left raw edge and marking off parallel lines at 2½ in. (6.35cm), 5 in. (12.7cm), 6½ in. (16.5cm), and 8 in. (20.3cm) using a dressmaker's pen and a ruler. Pin along the marked lines. Machine-stitch along each marked line, removing the pins as you work, to make the pocket section.

3 Position and pin the pocket section to the flannel-floral fabric section, bottom raw edges even. Measure and cut two 10-in. lengths (25.4cm) of red ribbon. Center and pin one end of each length to the top and the bottom, as shown. Machine-stitch the folded floral fabric along the sewn vertical lines to attach the pocket section to the layered section; set it aside.

4 Measure and cut a 10¼-in. (26cm) length of fur. Position and pin the ribbon part of the fur trim to the right side of one short side of the velvet rectangle (set aside in step 1). Machine-stitch, ½ in. (1.2cm) from the edge, being careful to avoid stitching over the fur.

5 Lay the pocket section flat, right side facing up. Lay the fur-trimmed velvet, wrong side up, on top, matching raw edges.

6 Pin the sections together, being careful to push the fur in between the fabric layers.

7 Machine-stitch the sections together, ⅜" (9.5mm) from the raw edges, leaving an opening for turning. Clip the corners, and turn the case to the right side. Whipstitch the opening closed by hand, using a threaded needle.

"What we hope
ever to do with ease,
we must first
learn to do
with diligence."

SAMUEL JOHNSON

red shoes

THE RED SHOES IS A FILM BASED ON A FAIRY TALE BY HANS CHRISTIAN ANDERSEN IN WHICH A DANCER FALLS IN LOVE AND BECOMES DISTRACTED FROM HER DEVOTION TO BALLET.

SKILL LEVEL
Intermediate

HOOK
F/5 (3.75mm) or size needed to obtain gauge

YARN
Classic Elite "Bazic Wool": 100% super-wash wool; [65yds. (59.0m)/51.7oz. (50g,)], in color #2958 Barn Red, 2 balls

NEEDLES
Hand-sewing

Tapestry

NOTIONS
4 ribbon roses

2 yds. (1.8m) thin beading elastic

2 yds. (1.8m) satin ribbon, ¼" (6.0mm) wide

Sewing thread

GAUGE
17 lkdc sts, 11 rows lkdc/sc pattern = 4" (10.1cm)

(continued on next page.)

A dancer's precious feet need to be treated with extra care and comfort, especially after being squeezed into pointe shoes. These slippers provide the welcome freedom, and warmth that soothes and relaxes hard-working feet. Crocheted in a soft cranberry-colored yarn, these comfy slip-ons are adorned with sweet ribbon roses and tied with ribbon streamers. The slipper design is inspired by the classic shape of the pointe shoe, yet unlike their ultra-snug fit, these slippers provide enough room to wiggle your toes and relax the muscles in your feet. Slip them on after a soak in an herbal footbath.

DESIGNED BY DEE STANZIANO

(continued from previous page.)

SPECIAL STITCHES

ExtSc: (extended single crochet) Insert hook into stitch, draw up loop, yo and draw through 1 loop loosely, yo and complete stitch as regular sc.

LkDC: (linked double crochet) Insert hook under horizontal bar in center of previous stitch, yo and draw up loop (2 loops on hook); insert hook into row st and draw up loop (3 loops on hook), yo and draw through 2 loops, yo again, and draw through remaining loops.

Ext LkDC: (extended linked double crochet) Insert hook under horizontal bar in center of previous stitch, yo and draw up loop (2 loops on hook); insert hook into row st and draw up loop (3 loops on hook), yo and draw through 1 loop loosely, yo and draw through 2 loops, yo again and draw through remaining loops.

Filet Style Increases: Some of the increases in this pattern are worked at the ends of rows into the new stitches just created, instead of into the row below. An extended st allows for an extra loop at the bottom of the st where a new st can be created "in thin air." So when you see an extended st, it's there to make room for the upcoming increase.

LkDC Inc: (linked double crochet increase) Work 2 LkDC stitches in same space.

LkTR: (linked triple crochet) Insert hook under top horizontal bar of previous stitch, yo and draw up loop (2 loops on hook); insert hook under bottom horizontal bar of same stitch,

insert hook into row st and draw up loop (4 loops on hook), yo and draw through 2 loops, yo again and draw through remaining loops.

Sc Dec: (single crochet decrease) Insert hook into stitch, draw up loop, insert hook into next stitch, draw up loop, yo and draw through all loops on hook.

The Linked Stitches create a solid fabric. Normally in crochet, when using double crochet (and taller) stitches, the first stitch of a new row is ignored so that the turning chain takes the place of the first stitch. This is not so with Linked Stitches. Work in the first stitch as directed, unless noted; do not work turning chains as stitches.

SIZING

Pattern will create one pair of relaxing slippers for a child's shoe size ranging from 11Y to 1Y. For longer feet, increase the length, repeating rows 2 and 3 based upon your measurement from the heel to the ball of foot.

Note: For directions to "Pas de Chat," the striped leg warmers shown on page 95, see page 41.

HEEL

Leaving at least a 12-in. tail for seaming, ch 23.

Row 1: Insert hook into 2nd ch from hook and draw up loop, insert hook in 4th ch from hook and draw up loop, work off like dc st, LkDC across (20 sts) turn.

Row 2: Ch 1, Sc across. (20 sts), turn.

Row 3: Ch 3, insert hook into 2nd ch from hook, draw up loop, turn work, insert hook in 1st st, draw up loop, yo draw through 2 loops, yo draw through last 2 loops, LkDC across. Turn. (20 sts)

Rows 4-11: Repeat Rows 2 and 3. (Remember, for a longer slipper, add length here—rep rows 2–3 until slipper reaches the ball of the foot on the wearer).

Row 12: Ch 1, sc across. Turn. (20 sts)

Row 13: Ch 4, insert hook into 2nd ch from hook and draw up loop, insert hook into 4th ch from hook and draw up loop, work off like dc; LkDC across to last st, Ext LkDC in last st, LkDC in bottom loop of st just created. Turn. (22 sts)

Row 14: Ch 2, 2 sc in 2nd ch from hook, sc across to last st, Ext Sc, work 2 sc in bottom loop of Ext Sc. Turn. (26 sts)

Row 15: Ch 4, insert hook into 2nd ch from hook and draw up loop, insert hook into 4th ch from hook and draw up loop, work off like dc; LkDC Inc in next st, LkDC across to 2nd to last st, LkDC Inc, Ext LkDC in last st, LkDC in bottom loop of Ext LkDC just created. Turn. (30 sts)

TOE:

In the next part of the piece the fabric will be joined, and worked in the round.

Rnd 1: Ch 1, sc across, join 1st st. to last with sl st (30 sts).

Rnd 2: Ch 3, insert hook into 2nd ch from hook and draw up loop, turn work, insert hook in next st, draw up loop, YO draw through 2 loops, YO, draw through last 2 loops, LkDC around. To join round, insert hook under horizontal bar. Then insert hook into top of 1st LkDC, YO, and draw through all loops on hook. Turn. (30 sts)

Rnd 3: Ch 1, *sc in next 4 sc, Sc dec, * repeat from around, join with sl st. (25 sts)

Rnd 4: Ch 3, insert hook into 2nd ch from hook and draw up loop, turn work, insert hook in next st, draw up loop, YO draw through 2 loops, YO draw through last 2 loops, LkDC in next 9 sts, YO, insert in horizontal bar, and draw up loop, insert hook into next st and draw up loop, YO, and remove two loops from hook three times, LkTC in next 4, insert hook in top and bottom horizontal bar of previous st and draw up loop, insert hook into next st and work of as dc, LkDC in next 9 sts. To join round, insert hook under horizontal bar, then insert hook into top of 1st LkDC, YO, and draw through all loops on hook. (25 sts) **Rnd 5:** Ch 1, turn, *sc in next 4 sts, Sc dec, repeat from * around, join with sl st. (20 sts) **Rnd 6:** Ch 1, turn, *sc in next 4 sts, Sc dec, repeat from * around, sc in last 2 sts, join with sl st (17 sts). Finish off.

Sew the toe and heal closed with a tapestry needle.

FINISHING TOUCHES:
Sew fabric flowers to the front of the toe section as shown.

Optional: *To give the slippers more of a "ballerina" look, trace the shape of the soles onto scraps of faux leather or suede and sew one to the bottom of each slipper.*

Optional: *Measure and cut two 1-yd. (91.4m) lengths of pretty ribbon, and thread one through the back of each slipper for lacing.*

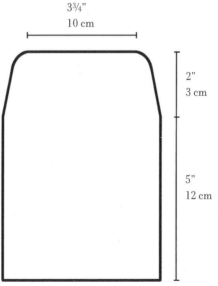

3¾"
10 cm

2"
3 cm

5"
12 cm

"Red Shoes" Diagram

6

CHAPTER

REHEARSING

The rehearsal schedules are posted, and the long, hard work of rehearsing a ballet begins. Rehearsals involve intense planning, preparation, and a collaboration of many talents. An inherent love for the dance becomes the heart of each practice and the motivation for perfection. Butterflies fill every stomach as dancers anticipate the choreographer's casting for the ballet. Once cast, dancers spend long, repetitious hours practicing the movements. Principals practice their beautiful *pas de deux*, and soloists and the corps rehearse together to get their timing precise. In the final days leading up to the performance, dancers often rehearse partially costumed in order to feel each movement and emotionally connect with their roles, while the costumer ensures that each gorgeous ensemble fits perfectly. Finally, just a day or so before the actual performance, a dress rehearsal is conducted, with everyone in full costume and makeup. This is the final chance for the choreographer, dancers, conductor, lighting designer, set designer, costumer, makeup artist, and stage technicians to make last-minute adjustments to perfect the production before opening in front of an audience. Rhinestones and sequins shimmer on the stage, enhancing each graceful movement of the dance, while the excitement of the real performance begins to set in. ✛

"No one can arrive from being talented alone.
God gives talent, work transforms talent into genius."
ANNA PAVLOVA

99

"*Nothing happens unless first a dream.*"

CARL SANDBURG

giselle

FOLK DANCES ARE INTEGRAL TO THE CHOREOGRAPHY OF MANY BALLETS
BECAUSE THE GESTURES, MOVEMENTS, AND COSTUMES OF PEASANT DANCES OFTEN
INSPIRE CHOREOGRAPHERS. THE BALLET *GISELLE* TAKES PLACE IN A PEASANT VILLAGE,
AND MANY OF THE COSTUMES AND DANCES FEATURED IN THIS BALLET ORIGINATE
IN THE TRADITION OF EUROPEAN FOLK DANCING AND DRESS.

MATERIALS

Artificial flowers with wired stems:

10 medium roses, pink

12–15 small roses, pink; yellow

12 bunches African violets, purple; pale lavender

5–8 impatiens, medium and dark pink

8 stems, lily of the valley

5 gypsophila ("baby's breath")

Assorted foliage (cut from flower stems)

2 yds. (1.8m) each of three narrow ribbons, in colors, as desired

Wire: 2 stem wires, 26 gauge; spool wire

Green floral tape

Wire cutters

Hot-glue gun and glue sticks

Scissors

Giselle, *a ballet that is a classic symbol of character and style in the peasant tradition, is the inspiration for this floral headdress. This sumptuous wreath of flowers includes roses that are framed by purple violets on one side and pale lavender lilacs on the other. Pale green leaves offset small pink and yellow roses, with white lilies peeping out from between them. When the headdress is worn, slender ribbons stream down the nape of the neck and adorn the dancer's back. The charm of this headdress is that it frames the beauty of the dancer's face, looking equally enchanting from both front and back. If you are fond of flowers, "Giselle" is a joy to make.*

making "giselle"

1 *Note: Measure the head circumference of the person who will be wearing the headdress.* Measure and cut two lengths of 26-gauge wire using the measurement, adding 2 in. (5.0cm) for overlap. Lay the wires together with ends even. Wind floral tape around the wires until they are concealed.

2 Make a hoop shape with the wire, overlapping and twisting the wires together at their ends to secure them.

3 Wrap the stem of an African violet around the wire hoop, as shown.

4 Referring to the photo above, continue to add the remaining flowers in the same way so that adjacent flowers touch and until the hoop is concealed. Add the foliage between the flowers, binding the stems with a separate length of wire to secure them to the hoop. Measure and cut four 18-in. (45.7cm) lengths of ribbon, and tie them to the floral wreath as shown. Optional: weave a pink-satin ribbon through the flowers, wrapping the ends once around the wreath and using hot glue to secure them.

Tip: When flowers come in small bunches, such as African violets, separate the blooms and add single flowers to the headdress for accent.

103

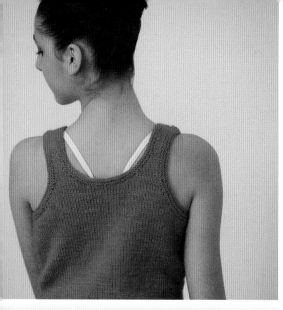

"Great dancers
are not great
because of
their technique,
they are great
because of
their passion."

PAMELA BROWN

arabesque

ORNAMENTAL AND BALANCED, THE ARABESQUE IS A POSE THAT OFTEN UNDERSCORES
A DRAMATIC MOMENT IN A BALLET. IN ACT III OF *SWAN LAKE*, ODILE, THE BLACK SWAN,
PERFORMS AN ARABESQUE AS SHE TRIES TO TAKE PRINCE SIEGFRIED'S
AFFECTIONS AWAY FROM ODETTE.

SKILL LEVEL
Experienced

SIZES
S (M, L)

FINISHED SIZE
Chest: 32 (34, 38)" [81.3
(86.36, 96.5)cm]

Length: 20 (21, 22)" [50.8
(53.3. 55.9)cm]

YARN
Patons "Classic Wool": 100%
merino wool; [223yds.
(204m)/3.5oz. (100g)], bright
blue, 2 balls

NEEDLES
1 pair size 4 (3.5mm)

1 pair size 3 (3.25mm) circular

NOTIONS
Stitch holder

GUAGE
20 sts and 30 rows = 4" (10.1cm)
in pattern.

ABBREVIATIONS
See page 174.

*In rehearsal, unlike class,
dancers can wear dancewear that
expresses their own individual
style and color preferences. This
vibrant blue woolen camisole
makes a vivid statement while
keeping you warm. It is knitted
with patterned stitching, and its
scalloped edge gently frames the
waist. The camisole can also be
worn at the end of rehearsal.
Although it requires some knitting
experience, it's fun to knit and
will make a great addition to
your wardrobe.*

DESIGNED BY LENA BUNEVITSKY

STITCH KEY

I	Knit
-	Purl
U	YO- Yarn Over
V	Knit, inserting the right needle into the previous row.
∧	Purl, inserting the right needle into the previous row.
↑	Sk2p (Slip 1, k2tog, pass slip st over the knit 2 tog)
ψ	Sk4p (Slip 1, k4tog, pass slip st over the knit 4 tog)

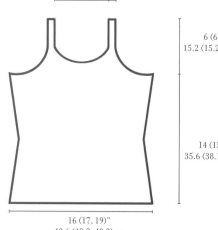

6 (6, 6)" — 15.2 (15.2, 15.2)cm ¾" 1.9cm

6 (6, 6)" — 15.2 (15.2, 15.2)cm

14 (15, 16)" — 35.6 (38.1, 40.6)cm

16 (17, 19)" — 40.6 (43.2, 48.3)cm

"Arabesque" Diagram

DESIGN PATTERN STITCHES

```
I V I                         -  ∧  -                    I V I - ∧ -   63
I V I                         U  ↑  U                    I V I - ∧ -   61
I V I                      U  I  ψ  I  U                 I V I - ∧ -   59
I V I                   I  I  U  ↑  U  I  I              I V I - ∧ -   57
I V I                   I  U  I  ↑  I  U  I              I V I - ∧ -   55
I V I                U  I  I  ψ  I  I  U                 I V I - ∧ -   53
I V I             I  I  I  U  ↑  U  I  I  I              I V I - ∧ -   51
I V I             I  I  U  I  ↑  I  U  I  I              I V I - ∧ -   49
I V I             I  U  I  I  ↑  I  I  U  I              I V I - ∧ -   47
I V I          U  I  I  I  ψ  I  I  I  U                 I V I - ∧ -   45
I V I       I  I  I  I  U  ↑  U  I  I  I  I              I V I - ∧ -   43
I V I       I  I  I  U  I  ↑  I  U  I  I  I              I V I - ∧ -   41
I V I       I  I  U  I  I  ↑  I  I  U  I  I              I V I - ∧ -   39
I V I       I  U  I  I  I  ↑  I  I  I  U  I              I V I - ∧ -   37
I V I    U  I  I  I  I  ψ  I  I  I  I  U                 I V I - ∧ -   35
I V I I I I I I U  ↑  U  I  I  I  I  I  I              I V I - ∧ -   11
I V I I I I I U  I  ↑  I  U  I  I  I  I                I V I - ∧ -    9
I V I I I I U  I  I  ↑  I  I  U  I  I  I               I V I - ∧ -    7
I V I I I U  I  I  I  ↑  I  I  I  U  I  I              I V I - ∧ -    5
I V I I U  I  I  I  I  ↑  I  I  I  I  U  I             I V I - ∧ -    3
I V I U  I  I  I  I  I  ↑  I  I  I  I  I  U            I V I - ∧ -    1
```

All WS rows work following the pattern (purl the purl stitches and knit
the knit stitches as they present themselves). Rows (1–11) repeat 3 times.

making "arabesque"

BACK

With size 4 needles, cast on 80 (86, 98) sts.
Beg with RS row, work in garter st for 4 rows, ending with a WS row.
Work 10 rows St st.

WAIST SHAPING

Beg on 11th row dec 1 st at each side (every 11th row) 3 times (74, 80, 92 sts).
Work even until piece measures 7" (17.7cm) from beg.
Beg on next row, inc 1 st at each side (every 11th row) 3 times (80, 86, 98 sts).
Work even until piece measures 14 (15, 16)" [35.6 (38.1, 40.6)cm] from beg.

SHAPE UNDERARMS

Row 1–2: BO 7 sts, work in pat to end of row.
Row 3–4: BO 5 sts, work in pat to end of row.
Row 5–6: BO 3 sts, work in pat to end of row.
Row 7–8: BO 2 sts, work in pat to end of row.
Beg row 9 dec 1 st at each side 5 times (36, 42, 54 sts).

SHAPE BACK NECK

Row 1: (RS) Knit across 18 (21, 27) sts. Turn. Place rem 18 (21, 27) sts on a stitch holder.
Row 2: BO 5 sts, purl to end of row.
Row 3: Knit across.
Row 4: BO 3 sts, purl to end of row.
Row 5: Knit across.
Beg row 6, (WS) dec 1 st at beg of WS row 5 times (5sts).
Continue to work even until piece measures 20 (21, 22)" [50.8 (53.3, 55.9)cm] from the beg.
BO.

Join yarn to rem 18 (21, 27) sts in the center of the piece (RS).
Row 1: BO 5 sts, knit to end of row.
Row 2: Purl across.
Row 3: BO 3 sts, knit to end of row.

Row 4: Purl across.
Beg row 5 (RS) dec 1 st at beg of RS row 5 times (5 sts).
Continue to work even until piece measures 20 (21, 22)" [50.8 (53.3. 55.9) cm] from the beg.
BO.

FRONT

With size 4 (3.5mm) needles, cast on 81 (87, 99) sts.
Beg with RS row, work in garter st for 4 rows, ending with WS row.
Start the "Design Pattern Stitches" on page 106, (RS) : k5 (8, 14) [p3, k3, yo, k5, sk2p, k5, yo, k3] 3 times, p3, k6 (9, 15).
Note: Each row you k5 (8), work the chart 3 times across the center of the front, k6 (9).

Continue to work the pat, and at the same time, beg with row 37, inc,1 st at each side every 4th row, 8 times. At the same time, beg row 53, (RS), m1 2sts before and 2 sts after working central pat.
Row 65: (RS) K to central pat, (p3, k3) 6 times, p3, k to end of row
Row 66: P to pat, (k3, p3) 6 times, k3, p to end of row

Rep rows 65 and 66 continuing to work side and m1 increases twice more.
Continue to work rows 65 and 66 omitting increases until piece measures 14 (15, 16)" [35.6 (38.1, 40.6)cm] from the beg.

SHAPE UNDERARMS

Follow the instructions for the same task under "Back."

SHAPE FRONT NECK

Row 1: (RS) Knit across 18 (21, 27) sts. Turn. Place rem 17 (20, 26) sts on a stitch holder.
Row 2: BO 5 sts, purl to end of row.
Row 3: Knit across.
Row 4: BO 3 sts, purl to end of row.

Row 5: Knit across.
Beg row 6(WS), dec 1 st at beg of WS row 5 times (5sts).
Continue to work until piece measures 20 (21, 22)" [50.8 (53.3, 55.9)cm] from the beg.
BO.
Join yarn to rem 17 (20, 26) sts in the center of the piece (RS).
Row 1: BO 4 sts, knit to end of row.
Row 2: Purl across.
Row 3: BO 3 sts, knit to end of row.
Row 4: Purl across.
Beg row 5 (RS), dec 1 st at beg of RS row 5 times (5 sts).
Continue to work until piece measures 20 (21, 22)" [50.8 (53.3, 55.9)cm] from the beg.
BO.

ASSEMBLY

Seam shoulder straps.

NECK BAND

Beg at right shoulder with size 3 circular needles, RS facing, pick up 168 (174, 186) sts along neckline. Put marker on first st.
Join and (k1 rnd, p1 rnd) 2 times.
BO on WS.

ARMBANDS

Beg at right shoulder with size 3 (3.25mm) circular needles, RS facing, pick up sts evenly along armhole edge.
Working back and forth in rows, knit 4 rows.
BO on WS.

FINISHING

Sew side seams.

"*Dancing can reveal all the mystery that music conceals.*"

CHARLES BAUDELAIRE

pirouette

IN THE CONTEXT OF A BALLET, A *DIVERTISSEMENT* IS A DIVERSION FROM THE STORY THAT ALLOWS A DANCER TO SHOW OFF HER VIRTUOSITY, OFTEN INCLUDING MANY, MANY *PIROUETTES*—COMPLETE TURNS OF THE BODY ON ONE FOOT, ON *POINTE* OR *DEMI-POINTE*.

SKILL LEVEL: Intermediate

BALLET PANTS

Legs are worked separately to waistband, then pieces are joined and waistband is worked in the round.

SIZES

S (M, L)

FINISHED MEASUREMENTS

Waist: 26 (30, 34)" [66 (76, 86)cm]

Length: 40" (1.0m) including the finished waistband

SIZING NOTE

If you would like to lengthen or shorten the pants, you may do so in the first 13" (33cm), before beginning leg shaping.

YARN

Royal Yarn Cashsoft DK: 50% extra fine merino, 40% acrylic microfibre, 10% cashmere; [142yds. (130m)/1¾ oz. (50g)], color #503, 10 (12, 13) balls

(continued on page 110)

During rehearsals at drafty, chilly theatres, it is comforting to be wrapped in a soft, comfortable, and luxurious outfit that helps you stay warmed up. This hand-knitted set is designed with an eyelet-patterned bodice that is delicately adorned with a white satin ribbon in the most feminine style. The pants, with their cable-knitted waistband, have a comfortable fit. "Pirouette" looks beautiful worn as an ensemble, or with the pieces worn separately along with other accessories.

DESIGNED BY STINA RAMOS

(continued from page 109)

NEEDLES
1 pair size 5 (3.75mm)

1 pair size 5 (3.75mm) 32" (80cm) circular (or size to obtain gauge)

NOTIONS
1½ yds. (1.37m) elastic, 1" (2.54cm) wide tapestry needle

GUAGE
24 sts and 32 rows = 4" (10.1cm) in St st

ABBREVIATIONS
See page 174.

SPECIAL ABBREVIATION
K2togTBL: knit 2 sts together through the back loop (left-slanting decrease)

PANTS
LEFT LEG
Cast on 96 (102, 108) sts.
Row 1: K1, p1 across.
Continue to work k1, p1 rib until cuff measures 1" (2.5 cm).

BODY OF LEG
Row 1: Change to St st, beginning with a knit row.
Work even in St st until piece measures 13" (33cm) or desired length from the beginning, ending with a WS row.
Note: If you want to change the length of the pants, lengthen or shorten here.

SHAPE LEG
(RS) Increase 1 st at each edge this row, then every 6th row, 21 times until you have 138 (144,150) sts.

Continue to knit even until piece measures 28" (71.1 cm) or desired length from the beginning, ending with a WS row.

SHAPING OF THE INSEAM
Row 1: (RS) K2togTBL, k across to last 2 sts, k2tog.
Row 2: P.

Rep rows 1–2 13 times or until you have 112 (118, 124) sts.

Change to dec every 4th row (8 times) until 96 (102, 108) sts remain.

Work even until piece measures 8 (8, 9)" [20.3 (20.3, 22.86)cm] from beginning of the decreases, ending on a WS row.

SHAPING THE RISE: INSEAM
(using short rows)

Row 1: (RS) K48 (51, 54), turn.
Row 2: P48 (51,54), turn.
Row 3: K46 (49,52), turn.
Row 4: P46 (49,52), turn.
Row 5: K44 (47,50), turn.
Row 6: P44 (47,50), turn.
Row 7: K42 (45,48), turn.
Row 8: P42 (45,48), turn.
Row 9: K40 (43,46), turn.
Row 10: P40 (43,46), turn.

Knit sts onto the circular needle and set aside.

RIGHT LEG
Work as for Left Leg until you finish inseam shaping, ending on a RS row.

SHAPING THE RISE
Row 1: (WS) P48 (51,54), turn.
Row 2: K48 (51,54), turn.
Row 3: P46 (49,52), turn.
Row 4: K46 (49,52), turn.
Row 5: P44 (47,50), turn.
Row 6: K44 (47,50), turn.
Row 7: P42 (45,48), turn.
Row 8: K42 (45,48), turn.
Row 9: P40 (43,46), turn.
Row 10: K40 (43,46), turn.

WAISTBAND
Knit pat 1x1 rib and cable pat (46sts).

Knit the piece onto the circular needle, making sure you have both backs side by side and RS facing. *Note: You'll be joining pieces to work in the round Start at the left side .*

Set-up Row: 1st piece: k1, p1 across to last 23sts, pm, p2, k2 across, (last st k1). 2nd front: k1, over 22 st, p2, k2, end p2 (foundation row for cable pat, over 46 sts), pm, k1, p1 across, end with p2tog (to adjust the rib pat, only on the 1st row).

Rnds 1-3: K to marker, k2, p2 to 2nd marker, k around.
Rnd 4: *(k2tog, but do not drop st off left ndl, k into 1st st on left ndl again, drop both off, p2) rep from * to end.

Continue pat for 4" (10.1cm). Next row, purl (folding edge row).
Follow pat for 1" (2.5cm).

BO all sts in pat.

Finishing: Sew front and back seams. Sew the leg seams.

Measure your waist. Cut a length of elastic 1" (2.5cm) shorter than waist measurement.

Sew the ends together. Start at the back seam. Fold the 1" (2.5cm) top of waistband/pants, over the elastic to WS and sew in place.

Helpful Hint: *attach the folding edge by sewing in the knit sts only; it is a great way to avoid the sts showing on the right side.*

SIZES

S (M, L)

FINISHED MEASUREMENTS

Bust: 34 (36, 38)" [86.36 (91.44, 96.52)cm]

Length (including strap): 20 (20, 21)" [50.8 (50.8, 53.34)cm]

YARN

Royal Yarn Cashsoft DK: 50% extra fine merino, 40% acrylic microfibre, 10% cashmere (142yds. (130m)/1¾ oz. (50g)], color # 503 6 (6, 7) balls, color # 503

NEEDLES

1 pair size 5 (3.75mm)

1 pair 5 (3.75mm) 16" (40cm) circular

1 pair 5 (3.75mm) 24" (60cm) circular

(or size to fit gauge)

GAUGE

24 sts and 32 rows = 4" (10.1 cm) St st

NOTIONS

2½ yds. (2.2m) ¼" (6.0mm) white satin ribbon

2 stitch holders

Extra needle (for 3-needle BO)

TOP

BACK

Cast on 98 (106, 112) sts, pm and begin working in the round

START WITH CABLE PATTERN

Rows 1- 3: (WS) K2, p2, across, end with k2.

Row 2: P2, k2 across, end with p2.

Row 4: * p2, k2tog but leave old sts on left needle, k again st closest to point of needle, slip old sts off,* rep from * to * end with p2.

Rep. rows 1–4, until work is 4 (4, 4½)" [10.2 (10.2, 11.4)cm] long. End with row 1, (WS).

RIBBON EYELET PATTERN

Rows 1-2: K.

Row 3: (RS) *k2 * yo, k2tog, p2 * rep from * to *. End with k2.

Rows 4-5: K.

Rows 6: (WS) P.

Row 7: K.

Row 8: (WS) P.

RIBBON EYELET PATTERN

1st Eyelet Pattern:

Row 1: (RS) K8, * yo, [sl1, k1, psso], k6 * rep from * to * end with k.

Row 2: P.

Row 3: K6 * k2tog, yo, k1, yo, [slip1, k1, psso], k3 * rep from * to * end with k7.

Rows 4-8: St st beginning with a p (WS) row.

2nd Eyelet Pattern:

Row 9: (RS) K4 * yo, [sl1, k1, psso], k6 * rep from * to * end with k4.

Row 10: P.

Row 11: K2 *k2tog, yo, k1, yo, [sl1, k1, psso], k3 * rep from * to * end with k3.

Rows 12-16: St st beginning with a p (WS) row.

Repeat rows 1–16 once more. Sizes S and M, end on row 14. Size L, end on row 16.

Rep Ribbon Eyelet Pattern once. Begin Cable pat again and work in pat until piece measures 11" (11, 11½)" [27.9 (27.9, 29.2)cm].

SHAPE ARMHOLE

Continue working in Cable pat, pm the 6th (6th, 7th) cable from each edge.

Working in pat, BO 7 sts at beg of the next 2 rows.

Continue to dec 1st at each armhole every RS row as follows; sl 1st st, k1, psso.

SHAPE ARMHOLE AND NECK EDGE

At the same time, when back measures 12 (12, 12½)" [30.5 (30.5, 31.8)cm] Place the 18 (18, 20) center sts of the row on a st holder. Continue working in pat back and forth on rem sts for back right side. Dec 1st each RS row both at neck edge and at armhole. Continue armhole and neck dec until you have only 2 sts on either side of the marked cable. Work even until strap measures 9" (22.8cm). Leave sts on holder.

Join yarn to back left neck edge and repeat neck and rep. above.

FRONT

Work as for back except begin neck edge shaping when front measures 11 (11, 11½)" [27.9 (27.9, 29.2)cm].

FINISHING

Join shoulder straps (front to back) with 3-needle BO.
Sew side seams.

EDGING

ARMHOLE

Pick up 80 sts evenly and work ribbon eyelet pat.

Row 1: P.

Row 2: *p2, yo k2tog, *rep from * to *.

Row 3: K.

Row 4: BO purlwise.

NECK EDGE

Start at the back, knit 18 (18, 20) sts on stitch holder onto needles, pick up 30 sts along neck edge evenly, knit the 18 (18, 20) sts from stitch holder (front), pick up 30 sts along neck edge, follow edging as for armhole.

"Pirouette" Diagrams

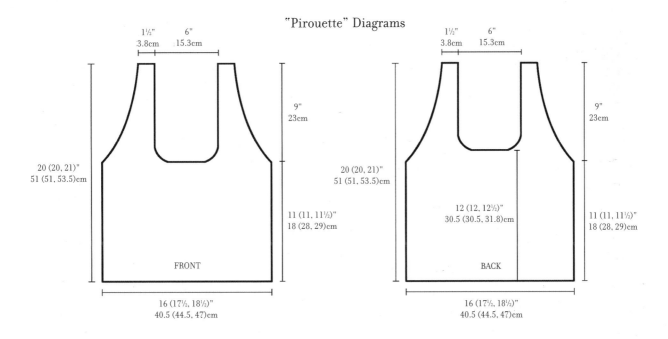

1½"
3.8cm

6"
15.3cm

9"
23cm

20 (20, 21)"
51 (51, 53.5)cm

11 (11, 11½)"
18 (28, 29)cm

FRONT

16 (17½, 18½)"
40.5 (44.5, 47)cm

1½"
3.8cm

6"
15.3cm

9"
23cm

20 (20, 21)"
51 (51, 53.5)cm

12 (12, 12½)"
30.5 (30.5, 31.8)cm

11 (11, 11½)"
18 (28, 29)cm

BACK

16 (17½, 18½)"
40.5 (44.5, 47)cm

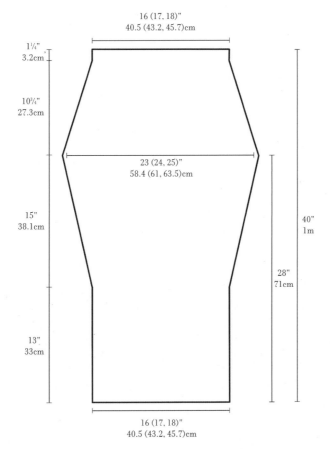

16 (17, 18)"
40.5 (43.2, 45.7)cm

1¼"
3.2cm

10¾"
27.3cm

23 (24, 25)"
58.4 (61, 63.5)cm

15"
38.1cm

40"
1m

28"
71cm

13"
33cm

16 (17, 18)"
40.5 (43.2, 45.7)cm

*"I'd rather learn from one bird how to sing than to teach
ten thousand stars how not to dance."*

E. E. CUMMINGS

chopin

MIKHAIL FOKINE, THE RUSSIAN CHOREOGRAPHER, BASED HIS BALLET *CHOPINIANA*
ON THE MUSIC OF CHOPIN. HE ALLOWED THE POETIC AND LYRICAL QUALITIES OF THE MUSIC
TO DICTATE THE DANCE MOVEMENTS AND LEFT OUT THE USUAL SPECTACULAR FEATS IN
THE *PAS DE DEUX*, THINKING THEY WOULD NOT BE IN CONCERT WITH THE TEMPO
AND SENSIBILITY OF THE BEAUTIFUL WALTZ.

MATERIALS

Art: "Star" (See page 117.)

¼ yd. (22.8cm) rayon velvet, dark blue

¼ yd. (22.8cm) rayon lining, light purple

Matching thread

Fabric marker

Seed beads, one vial each of iridescent blue and silver

Ruler

Scissors

Straight pins

Beading needle

Sewing machine

Listening to music on an i-Pod™ during rehearsal breaks helps dancers unwind, or even mentally practice their steps while they rest. Here, a special pouch is the perfect way to both decorate and protect an i-Pod. Made in shimmering velvet, the pouch is decorated with a star motif. The design elements are symbolic: the deep blue velvet represents a nocturnal sky, and the star, depicted in iridescent seed beads, represents the wishes and aspirations that ballet stars tend to inspire.

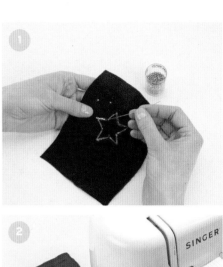

making "chopin"

1. Measure and cut two 3-in.-by 5½-in. (7.6cm x 13.9cm) rectangles from the velvet and two same-size rectangles from the lining fabric; set all rectangles aside except one velvet rectangle. Use a fabric marker to trace the star motif onto the center of the velvet rectangle. Use a beading needle to sew beads along the marked line, adding single beads around the central star if desired.

2. Lay the beaded rectangle on the second velvet rectangle, right sides facing and raw edges even. Pin and machine-stitch the rectangles together along three sides, keeping one short side unsewn.

3. Lay the rectangles of lining together, right sides facing and raw edges even. Pin and machine-stitch the rectangles together along three sides, keeping one short side unsewn. Trim the corners as shown. Turn the lining pouch to the right side.

4. Turn over a ¼-in. (6.0mm) hem on the top opening of the velvet pouch.

5. To make the strap, measure and cut a 1½-in. by 8-in. (3.81cm x 20.3cm) rectangle from velvet. Fold the rectangle in half lengthwise and sew the length, a scant ¼ in. (6.0mm) from the raw edge. Turn the tube to the right side. Use a threaded needle to sew one opening closed. Position and pin the strap to the velvet at the top of the pouch.

6. Slip the lining onto the velvet pouch, as shown, sandwiching the strap between the lining and the velvet.

7. Machine- or hand-stitch the lining and velvet pouches together a scant ¼ in. (6.0mm) from the folded edges.

8. Sew on a snap, one part to the strap and one part to the pouch, as shown.

"Chopin" Pattern

CHAPTER

7

PERFORMING

As dancers arrive at the stage door, a tangible sense of excitement fills the theater. Backstage, dancers frantically apply makeup, fix costumes, find missing props, and warm up. Bright lights around the mirrors illuminate the performers as they get ready, while sounds of the orchestra warming up float backstage. In the darkened wings, a narrow swath of light from the stage reveals dancers watching their fellow performers, quietly cheering at every finish. They calm their own nervousness by interlocking their fingertips with another dancer's in the traditional good-luck custom. When the music finally strikes those familiar notes—their cue— these dancers enter the glowing stage, bathed in the spotlight. They demonstrate their finest in technique and choreography, which they have spent so many hours perfecting, revealing their souls as they let the music flow through them. All inhibitions released, all energy focused on the variation, the dancers perform with pure joy and exhilaration. They gaze out into the dark sea of faces with that fleeting feeling of utter freedom and satisfaction. The magnetism of their performance creates a thrill in the audience that is rewarded with cheers, applause, and flowers. As the curtain falls, the dancers feel a bittersweet mixture of accomplishment and sadness at the conclusion of their effort. That is, until the next performance, when spirits soar again as the curtain rises. ✛

"...I have danced, at any given time, for about ten people...They were the ones that left the theatre forever different from the way they were when they came in. All of my long, long life, I have danced for those ten."

RUTH ST. DENIS

dew drop

"DEW DROP" IS THE NAME OF ONE OF THE SOLOISTS IN BALANCHINE'S *THE NUTCRACKER* BALLET. PERFORMED EVERY CHRISTMAS, THE BALLET SHOWS THE BEAUTIFUL DEW DROP IN A COSTUME AND TIARA THAT SPARKLE IN THE STAGE LIGHTS AND SHIMMER LIKE DEW DROPS AS SHE PERFORMS HER INTRICATE FOOTWORK, DAZZLING THE AUDIENCE.

MATERIALS

82 bicone crystals, 4mm

16 crystal rondelles:

    10 gold, 5mm

    6 faceted, 7mm

5 teardrop crystals, 11mm

2 crimp beads, small, silver

2 crimp covers

Beading wire, 26 gauge

3" (7.6cm) silver chain, 4mm links, with decorative ball at end

Lobster clasp, 7mm

Wire cutters

3 pairs of pliers: crimping; round-nose; and chain-nose

Ruler

Light falls gently on the crystals on this necklace, stirring a blaze of rainbow color from each gem. Like the dew drops on flowers in early morning, the teardrop crystals on this choker reflect a delicate pattern of light that sparkles on the neck as the dancer's movement brings the necklace into different points of contact with the stage lights. Elegant in its iridescent simplicity, the "Dew Drop" choker is a joy to create.

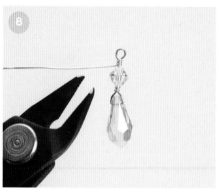

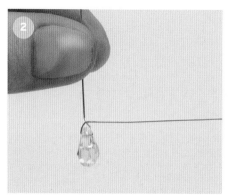

making "dew drop"

1 Lay out five teardrop crystals and five 4.0mm bicones. Measure and cut five ⁵⁄₈-in. (15.0mm) lengths of wire. To make one crystal pendant, insert the end of one wire through a teardrop crystal. Cross the wires as shown.

2 Use your fingers to bend one wire at a 90-deg. angle.

3 Wrap the wire (bent in step 2) around the vertical wire stem two times. Use the wire cutters to snip off the excess wire.

4 Insert the wire stem through a 4.0mm bicone crystal. Then use the chain-nose pliers to bend the wire at a 90-deg. angle ⅛ in. (3.0mm) above the bicone crystal.

5 Grasp the wire stem ⅛ in. (3.0mm) above the bend, using the round-nose pliers. Rotate the pliers toward the bend, and use your fingers to bend the wire around the jaw of the pliers.

6 Cross the wire in front of the wire stem to make a loop.

7 Grasp the loop with the chain-nose pliers, and use the round-nose pliers to wrap the wire around the stem, moving from the loop down toward the bicone crystal.

8 Use the wire cutters to snip off the excess wire. Then use the chain-nose pliers to squeeze the cut end of wire flush against the stem. Repeat steps 1–8 to make four more crystal pendants with wrapped loops. Set the pendants aside.

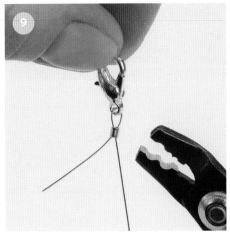

"Dew Drop" Beading Diagram

9 Measure and cut a 15-in. (38.1cm) length of wire. Thread the wire through a crimp bead, the lobster clasp, and back through the crimp bead, using the crimping tool to secure the bead. Slip the crimp bead inside the open halves of the crimp cover, and squeeze the halves together to trap the bead inside.

10 Thread on a crystal bicone, making certain the short end of wire is inside the crystal bead. Referring to the "Beading Diagram," thread on 25 bicones (for a total of 26), adding one gold rondelle, one faceted rondelle, one gold rondelle, three bicones, one pendant, three bicones, one gold rondelle, one faceted rondelle, one gold rondelle, three bicones, one pendant, three bicones, one gold rondelle, one faceted rondelle, three bicones, and one pendant, which marks the center of the necklace. Continue beading, reversing the order of beads, and ending with a bicone.

11 Thread the end of the wire through a crimp bead, the end link in the decorative chain, and back through the crimp bead. Use the crimping pliers to secure the crimp bead. Enclose the crimp bead in a crimp cover as in step 9. Trim the wire, leaving a short piece and tucking it into the last beads.

"Dancing is my gift and my life. God gave me this gift to bring delight to others. I am haunted by the need to dance. It is the purest expression of every emotion, earthly and spiritual. It is happiness."

ANNA PAVLOVA

pavlova

ANNA PAVLOVA, ONE OF THE WORLD'S GREATEST BALLERINAS, HAD A SPECIAL SPIRIT FULL OF INTENSITY, PASSION, AND A GRACEFULNESS THAT MADE EVERY MOVE SHE DANCED MAGICAL AND MEMORABLE. SHE TRAVELED THE WORLD PERFORMING WITH THE TRUEST ARTISTRY.

MATERIALS

Wire-and-mesh tiara base, 6 ½" (16.5cm) dia., 1½" (3.9cm) high

½-yd. (45.7cm) length single rhinestone strand, 2mm wide

½ yd. (45.7cm) lattice-style rhinestones, 4mm wide

14 square rhinestones, 5mm

8 round pearls, 5mm dia.

3 rhinestone buttons, 13mm

Permanent jewelry adhesive

Tape measure

Scissors

Wire cutters

OPTIONAL

Silver wire, 32 gauge; toothpick

"Tiara" is synonymous with the word "princess," and in ballet, principal ballerinas wear them in leading roles. Reminiscent of the royal courts where ballet originated, the sparkle of the regal tiara has enchanted audiences for centuries. Here, a plain base used by theatrical costumers and designed for the stage is decorated with rhinestones and pearls. "Pavlova" acquires a magnificent brilliance under stage lights, adding to the magical atmosphere of a ballet.

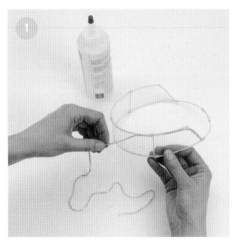

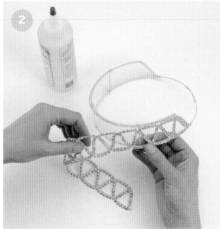

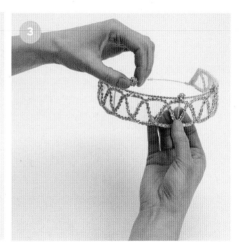

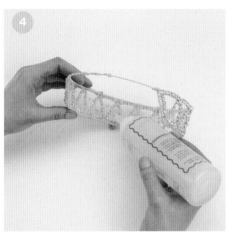

making "pavlova"

1 Measure the length of the tiara at the top edge of the crown section. Use that measurement to cut a length of the single strand of 2mm rhinestones, using a ruler and wire cutters. Position and secure the rhinestones to the top edge of the tiara, using permanent adhesive; let the adhesive dry. *Optional: For more security, use wire to lash the rhinestone strands to the mesh.*

2 Lay the lattice-style rhinestones parallel with and touching the rhinestones glued in step 1. Secure the lattice of rhinestones to the tiara using permanent adhesive; let the adhesive dry. *Optional: For more security, use wire to lash the rhinestone strands to the mesh.*

3 Position and glue a rhinestone button to the center of the top edge of the tiara as shown. Repeat to secure two more buttons, each approximately 2¼" (5.7cm) from the center button. Add the pearls and single rhinestones as shown, alternating them between the triangular, rhinestone-bordered spaces.

4 Turn the tiara to the wrong side. Apply a small dab of adhesive through the woven mesh and onto the back of each rhinestone button, individual rhinestone, and pearl. Let the glue dry. *Note: Clean off excess glue with a toothpick.*

127

"We ought to dance with rapture that we might be alive and part of the living incarnate cosmos."

D.H. LAWRENCE

aurora

ONE OF THE MOST FAMOUS ADAGIOS IN BALLET HISTORY IS THE "ROSE ADAGIO,"
FROM *THE SLEEPING BEAUTY*, IN WHICH PRINCESS AURORA DANCES WITH FOUR PROSPECTIVE
SUITORS, EACH OF WHOM PRESENTS HER WITH A ROSE. THE CROWNING ACHIEVEMENT
OF THIS ADAGIO IS THE MOMENT AURORA BALANCES EFFORTLESSLY IN ATTITUDE
AS EACH SUITOR SLOWLY PROMENADES HER.

MATERIALS

Purchased adult tutu

Layout diagram: "Aurora"
(See page 131.)

2 yds. (1.8m) gold braid,
½" (1.3cm) wide

Gold thread

Straight pins

Hand-sewing needle

Tape measure

Hot-fix rhinestones, pink,
6mm

Hot-fix tool for gems

Scissors

GENERAL DIRECTIONS

Position and pin the braided
trim in a pleasing design on
your bodice, using the
"Aurora Layout Diagram" as
a guide. Overlap the ends,
and trim off the excess braid.
Use a hand-sewing needle
with matching thread to
secure the trim to the
bodice. *Optional: Use the
rhinestone setter to add rhinestones to the braid.*

*The tutu was originally designed
with a tulle skirt long enough to
grace the calves of a dancer; this
style is called the "romantic" tutu.
It evolved to a shorter skirt, named
the "classic" tutu, that enables the
audience to better see the ballerina's beautiful footwork. Here, the
bodice of an exquisitely elegant
classic tutu, in a pancake-style, is
adorned with an elegant design
crafted for the role of Princess
Aurora in* The Sleeping Beauty. *If
you have a plain tutu and wish to
decorate it so that it resembles our
"Aurora," all you need to do is
add loops of intricate gold braid
and shimmering pink rhinestones,
as shown on the opposite page.
The design will glisten and sparkle
when light shines upon it.*

DESIGNED BY RIMA DAY

BEGIN HERE

"Aurora" Layout Diagram

131

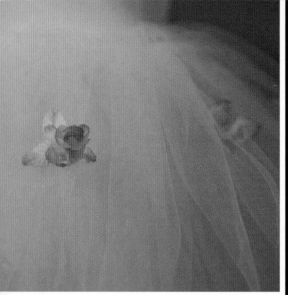

*"To watch
us dance is
to hear our
hearts speak."*
HOPI INDIAN SAYING

waltz of the flowers

IN SOME PRODUCTIONS OF *THE SLEEPING BEAUTY*, "THE WALTZ OF THE FLOWERS" IS
PERFORMED BY CHILDREN WHO DANCE WITH COLORFUL GARLANDS OF BEAUTIFUL FLOWERS.

MATERIALS

Purchased tutu, child's size

12 artificial roses with wire stems, approximately ½" (1.3cm) wide

Wire cutters

Fabric glue

Matching thread

Hand-sewing needle

Scissors

A beginning ballerina feels heavenly when enveloped in a cloud of pink tulle as she makes her stage debut wearing her first tutu. The event can mark the first step on the path to a dance career. Here, "Waltz of the Flowers" is a confection of tulle that is perfect for such a momentous occasion. Reminiscent of the Degas sculpture called "The Dancer," this tutu is beautiful in its simplicity. All you do is decorate a store-bought tutu with a scattering of pink roses, saving one to place on the bodice (close to the heart).

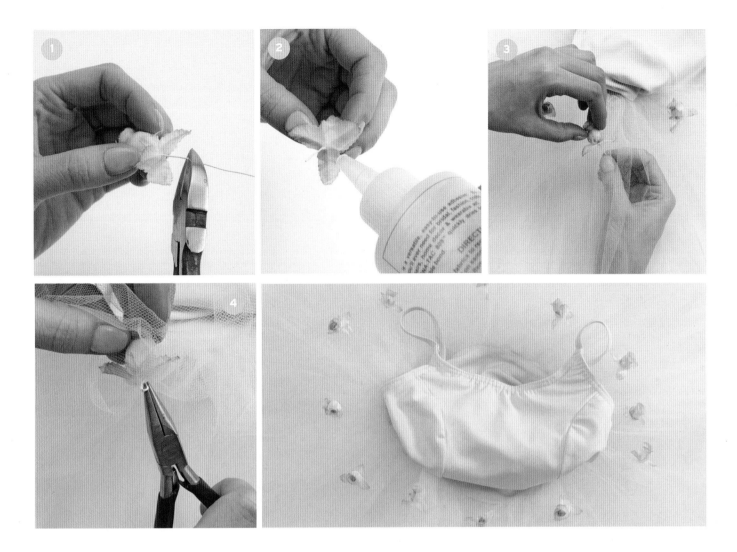

making "waltz of the flowers"

1 Snip off the excess stems of the roses, using the wire cutters, leaving a ¼-in. (3.0mm) long stub.

2 Turn one rose to the back, and apply a dab of glue to the center of the bloom near the stem.

3 Place one hand under the tulle in a position near the waistband where you wish to attach a rose. Hold the rose from step 2 with the other hand, and insert the wire stub through the weave in the tulle, grabbing the stub with your hand and pulling the rose flush with the tulle.

4 Use pliers to bend the wire into a small loop, and hide it under the rose. Continue to add roses in a random pattern, as shown or as desired. Let the glue dry.

"Take the stage and command it.
You have the talent, now let it possess you.
Audiences come to the theatre to see people
obsessed by what they do."

RUDOLF NUREYEV

mazurka

A MAZURKA IS A POLISH FOLK DANCE PERFORMED IN TRIPLE METER.
THE DANCE ORIGINATED IN THE AREA AROUND WARSAW, POLAND.
THE DANCE IS INCORPORATED INTO MANY BALLETS.

MATERIALS

Assorted ribbons:

1 yd. (91.4cm) pink brocade, 1⅜" (3.4cm) wide

1 yd. (91.4cm) dark-pink satin, 1" (2.5cm) wide

1 yd. (91.4cm) light-pink satin, 1" (2.5cm) wide

1 yd. (91.4cm) rose silk, ⅜" (9.0mm) wide

1 yd. (91.4cm) striped gros grain, 1" (2.5cm) wide

1 yd. (91.4cm) light pink gros grain, 1" (2.5cm) wide

1 yd. (91.4cm) pink brocade, ⅜" (9.0mm) wide

Poster board

¼ yd. (22.8cm) fusible webbing, light-weight

½ yd. (45.7cm) white cotton fabric for interfacing

½ yd. (45.7cm) lining fabric, pink

Matching thread

Hand-sewing needle

Dress zipper, 9" (22.8cm) long, pink

Ruler

Scissors

Household iron

Sewing machine

Life in the ballet theater is interwoven with many beautiful elements—performers, choreography, costumes, makeup, scenery, music, and lighting, much like this woven makeup case, which is made by weaving together ribbons that harmonize with one another. Makeup is an important component of ballet theatre and contributes greatly to the illusions that make up a ballet story. Stage makeup is applied more dramatically than ordinary makeup to exaggerate the dancer's features so that the audience in the back of the theatre and balcony can better see the dancer's expressive face. To organize your makeup, make our elegant "Mazurka" case.

DESIGNED BY BETH VOGL

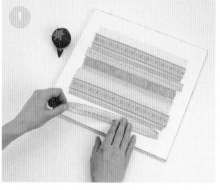

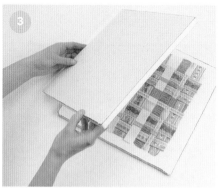

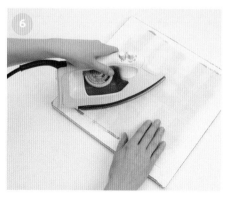

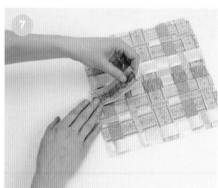

making "mazurka"

1 Lay a piece of poster board on your work surface. Measure and cut approx. 22 11-in. (27.9cm) lengths of ribbon. Referring to the weaving diagram, arrange any 10-12 ribbons horizontally on the board in a random pattern until they measure 11 in. (27.9cm) high. Use straight pins to secure the ends of each ribbon.

2 Using the weaving diagram as a guide, weave any 10-12 ribbons through those arranged in step 1 in a random pattern until the weaving measures approximately 9½ in. by 11 in. (24.1cm x 27.9cm), making certain the weaving is tight and the ribbons are parallel. Reposition the pins, if necessary. *Note: The ribbon ends can be trimmed as necessary once the weaving is finished.*

3 Lay the second sheet of poster board on top of woven ribbons. Hold the "sandwich," and flip it over. Lift off the poster board to reveal the woven fabric, wrong side facing up.

4 Use scissors, to trim the fusible webbing to the size of the woven-ribbon fabric, approximately 9½ in. by 11 in. (24.1cm x 27.9cm). Place the fusible webbing, adhesive side down, on top of the woven ribbons, and use an iron to adhere it according to instructions on the package.

5 Peel off the lining paper to reveal the back of the weaving. *Note: The back of the woven ribbons will have a smooth and dry film of adhesive on it. This adhesive will help the lining fabric adhere, thereby stabilizing the weaving.*

6 Cut a piece of lining fabric the size of your woven piece, approximately 9½ in. by 11 in. (24.1cm x 27.9cm). Position the lining over the fusible webbing, and iron it to adhere it to the woven-ribbon rectangle. Machine-stitch along the ribbon edges to secure them.

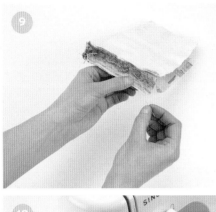

7 Lay the woven rectangle lengthwise, lining side up. Fold the bag in half, and use pins to mark the fold at each side. Lay the rectangle flat again. Fold and press ½ in. (1.2cm) on each side of the center fold to indicate the 1-in.-wide (2.5cm) base of the bag. Measure and cut a piece of brocade ribbon one-half the width of the woven piece, and pin it to the center of one side as shown.

8 Fold up and pin the sides of the woven rectangle to the sides of the ribbon, right sides together, to make the gusset.

9 Use a threaded needle to baste the ribbon to the sides of the bag.

10 Cut one 11-in. (27.9cm) length of brocade ribbon to make the second gusset with a loop extension. Position and

pin the ribbon to the opposite side of the bag, folding over the ribbon to make a loop handle. Baste it in place ¼ in. (6.0mm) from the edge.

11 Machine-stitch both gussets in place, ¼ in.(6.0mm) from the edge.

12 Cut three pieces of pink lining fabric, two approx. 1½ in. by 5½ in. (3.8cm x 14.0cm), and one 9½ in. by 11 in. (24.1cm x 27.9cm). Use them to make the bag lining, following steps 7–9 to put in both gussets. Turn over a ⅜-in. (9.0mm) hem.

13 Insert the bag's lining into the bag, wrong sides together. Hand-stitch the lining into the bag around the opening.

14 Follow the directions on the zipper package to install a zipper along the opening of the bag.

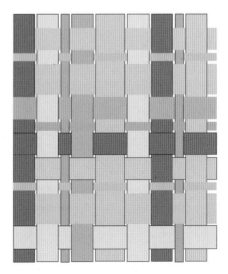

"Mazurka" Weaving Diagram

CHAPTER

PRESERVING MEMORIES

Every live performance creates unique memories for the dancers. Even when the ballet itself is the same, the experience is distinctive. The theatre, the music, and the audience—they all transform in the light of the stage, augmented by backstage antics, frantic moments, missteps, and the perfect arabesque. To remember these moments, dancers take pictures, press flowers received, and save programs, ticket stubs, and notes from friends. Photographs and memorabilia tell a good part of the story, but the most accurate depictions are in journals, written while the memories are still fresh and vivid. All of these things, as well as the emotions they evoke, can be preserved and cherished for years thereafter in a scrap-book-like amalgam. Dancers can not only revisit these fleeting and joyous parts of life, they can share them with others. ✚

"On with the dance! Let joy be unconfined."

LORD BYRON

141

"There was a star danced, and under that was I born."

WILLIAM SHAKESPEARE

Much Ado About Nothing

libretto

THE BALLET BEGAN IN ITALY, WAS DEVELOPED IN FRANCE, AND REACHED ACROSS TO RUSSIA. "LIBRETTO," A DIMINUTIVE OF THE ITALIAN WORD *LIBRO*, WHICH MEANS "BOOK," REFERS TO THE STORY OF AN OPERA, A BALLET, OR OTHER DRAMATIC MUSICAL WORK.

MATERIALS

Purchased photo album* with detachable covers, one with a picture window (*Note: The covers and sheets of photo paper on our album are held together by screws.*)

½ yd. (45.7cm) red velvet

Ribbon, trims, and beads, as desired.

SHOWN ON OUR ALBUM

½ yd. (45.7cm) gold lace trim, 1½" (3.8cm) wide

½ yd. (45.7cm) red-and-gold brocade ribbon, 1" (2.5cm) wide

1 yd. (91.4cm) red velvet ribbon, ¼" (6.0mm) wide

¼ yd. (22.8cm) gold metallic ribbon, ½" (1.2cm) wide

Bicone crystals: 24 red, 5mm; 24 silver, 5mm

Spray adhesive

Permanent fabric glue

Ruler

Marking pencil

Scissors

The czars of Imperial Russia loved the ballet. They had a special box at St Petersburg's famous Mariinsky Theatre that was decorated with red velvet, shimmering chandeliers, and ornate gilded moldings that glowed. It was a custom that the czar would present a gift of a diamond to the principal ballerina in appreciation of her fine performance. This album's opulence is reminiscent of the Imperial style, which used gold, rubies, diamonds, and pearls to frame favorite photographs. Long after the applause has faded, you can preserve the memories of past performances in an album such as "Libretto."

making "libretto"

Note: Work in a well-ventilated space.

1 Detach the covers from your album. Lay the velvet flat, wrong side up. Center the back cover on the velvet, opening up and flattening the folded spine. Mark and cut a 1-in.-wide (2.5cm) flap of velvet on all four sides.

2 Lay the velvet, wrong side up, and the cover, right side up, on a protected surface. Spray adhesive on the velvet and the cover. Center the cover, glue side down, on the velvet. Lay the cover flat, wrong side up. Fold over and glue the long flaps to the cover as shown.

3 For easement of the velvet at the folds in the cover, cut out a narrow rectangle of velvet as shown.

4 For easement at the flaps on the short sides of the cover, cut out a rectangle of velvet, leaving a ½ in. wide (1.2cm) flap. (See 4a for detail.)

144

5 Use scissors to trim across the corners of velvet. (See 5a for detail.)

6 Fold over and glue a ¼-in.-wide (6.0mm) flap at each trimmed corner. (See 6a for detail.)

7 Fold over and glue the short flap to the cover. Repeat the steps to glue the second short flap at the opposite side.

8 Glue a length of ½-in.-wide (1.2cm) gold ribbon to one short and two long sides of the cover, centering the ribbon over the raw edge.

9 Measure and cut a 10-in. (25.4cm) length of red ribbon. Center and glue the ribbon to the cover as shown; set the back cover aside.

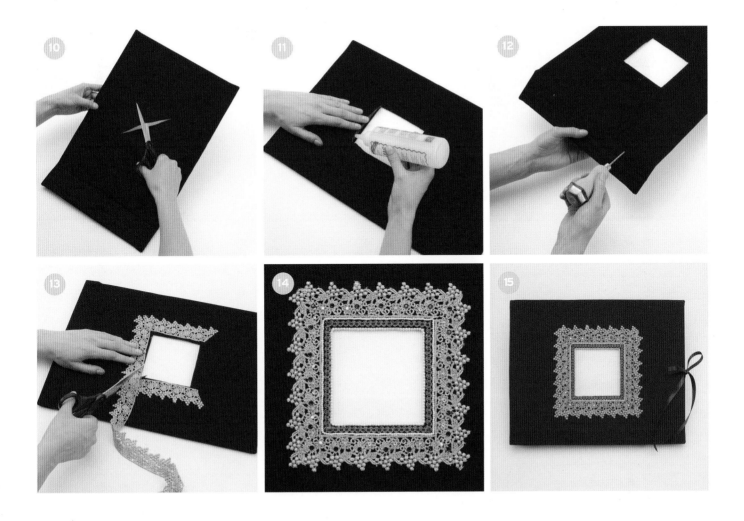

making "libretto" continued...

10 Repeat steps 1–9 to apply velvet and ribbons to the front cover. Then mark an "X" on the velvet within the center cutout "window" section of the cover, beginning and ending the diagonal lines ³⁄₈ in. (9.0mm) from the inside corners of the window. Cut along the marked lines.

11 Trim off the triangular-shaped flaps, leaving a ¹⁄₄-in.-wide (6.0cm) flap of velvet. Run a very light, thin bead of glue along the wrong side of one trimmed flap, then press the glued edge to the edge of the window. Repeat to glue the remaining flaps.

12 Insert the awl through the velvet and into one screw hole to make a hole in the fabric. Apply a dab of glue to the raw edges of velvet using your fingers; let the glue dry. Repeat at the second screw hole.

13 Lay the front cover flat. Position and cut four lengths of the 1¹⁄₂-in-wide (3.8cm) gold lace trim to decorate the sides of the window, cutting the lace ends on an angle so that they abut one another. Glue down the lace.

14 Continue to position and glue the remaining ribbons and rhinestones in positions as desired; let the glue dry.

15 Assemble the album, and tie the red velvet ribbons in a bow to close it.

> *"Every man's memory is his private literature."*
>
> ALDOUS HUXLEY

encore

AT THE END THEIR MAGNIFICENT PERFORMANCE IN *SWAN LAKE* AT THE VIENNA STATE
OPERA BALLET IN 1964, RUDOLF NUREYEV AND MARGOT FONTEYN RECEIVED 89 CURTAIN
CALLS, SETTING A WORLD RECORD IN ENCORES. IT IS NOT UNCOMMON FOR AUDIENCES TO ASK
FOR AN ENCORE, OR ADDITIONAL PERFORMANCE, WHEN THEY HAVE BEEN PARTICULARLY
PLEASED BY WHAT THEY HAVE EXPERIENCED.

MATERIALS

Collected souvenirs, as
desired

Poster board, size as
desired

Glue stick

Optional: box, size
as desired

*Memories come back to life when
we see sentimental souvenirs that
we have saved from special events
or experiences. One way to hold
the reminders in one place for all
time is to make a collage. By col-
lecting and aesthetically arranging those things that are touch-
stones of past events, we can relive
some of the emotions and remember the details of the original experience. "Encore" is a fitting name
for a collage filled with memori-
bilia—photos, postcards, trinkets,
and small mementos, including a
signed pointe shoe. The collage is
made to fit inside a memory box
with a hinged lid, but whether
displayed inside a box or on a
wall, this souvenir collage will
bring back memories of the joy and
excitement of being a part of the
world of ballet.*

making "encore"

The art of collage has been practiced for centuries. Much like today's scrapbooking, here, favorite mementos are arranged and glued to a single sheet of posterboard. When you make your collage, let your imagination guide you. There are no set rules for making a collage although there are some general guidelines that can maximize the appearance of each treasure. When you have finished your collage, you can display it on a bulletin board or place it inside a box of any kind. If you decide to use a box, cut your poster board to fit inside before you begin work. The box can be as ordinary as a shoebox or something as elaborate as the featured box with a hinged glass door.

Here are a few things to keep in mind:

• The process of arranging the elements of your collage should be very free to allow your creative imagination to flourish; the charm of a collage is the spontaneity with which you arrange the elements.

• Select a theme for your collage such as "Attending My First Ballet," "My First Recital," or any other idea that appeals to you. Or begin your collection with no predetermined idea, simply adding single elements to your collage as you go along.

• Collect souvenirs that have special meaning, touch some memory, or help tell a personal story. Here are some suggestions of items that might be fun to add to your collage: a ticket stub from a ballet; a dance program; autographs; postcards; pictures from magazines and the Internet; scraps of ribbon and trim; tiles from a board game that spell out a special word; a *pointe* shoe; and anything else that has meaning to you.

• Lay out your collection of souvenirs on a clean, flat surface. If you are going to install your collage in a box, measure and cut your poster board to fit. Then begin your collage by arranging all the items on the poster board, switching items around as you wish. If necessary, cut out any images or parts of images that you wish to use in a smaller size. Also don't forget to save the scraps. The small elements can add impact to the overall look of your collage.

• When you are designing your collage, you will notice that a kind of layering naturally takes place. To affix your souvenirs, use a glue stick or a hot-glue gun. Begin by gluing the pieces that you wish to see in the background. Step away from the arrangement to make certain you like the look. Then, glue down the other elements to the collage, one at a time, building another layer of souvenirs in front of the background elements.

• If you intend to fit your collage inside a box, install the collage when you are happy with your arrangement of items and the glue has dried. Then stand the box upright. If you have larger, three-dimensional items, use the side of the box that rests on the surface for a "shelf."

• Continue to add more souvenirs to your collage if you wish, or simply begin the collage-making process again, making a second or third collage as your collection of sentimental souvenirs grows.

"You've gotta dance like there's nobody watching, love like you'll never be hurt. Sing like there's nobody listening, and live like it's heaven on earth."

WILLIAM W. PURKEY

nutcracker angel

ONE OF THE MOST POPULAR AND MEMORABLE BALLETS IS *THE NUTCRACKER*. GEORGE
BALANCHINE'S VERSION OFFERS YOUNG DANCERS THE OPPORTUNITY TO DANCE MANY ROLES.
ONE SPECIAL INTRODUCTORY ROLE IS THAT OF THE NUTCRACKER ANGELS WHO APPEAR AT
THE BEGINNING OF THE SECOND ACT, DANCING ON STAGE WITH THE PRINCIPAL DANCER WHO
DANCES THE ROLE OF THE SUGAR PLUM FAIRY.

MATERIALS

Patterns: Nutcracker Angel
(*See pages 154 and 155.*)

Coin, 1¼" (3.17cm) in dia.

Wooden skewer, ⅜" (9.0mm) dia.

2 wooden beads, ⅝" (1.5cm) dia.

White satin ribbon, 4" (10.0cm)
wide

½ yd. (45.7cm) braided trim,
¼" (6.0mm) wide

1 pkg. metallic stars

Fabric glue

Acrylic paint: flesh; brown;
dark pink

Card stock

1 vial of gold micro-glitter

White thread

Batting

Paintbrush

Ruler

Utility knife

Scissors

Straight pins

Hand-sewing needle

As the curtain rises for the second act of The Nutcracker, *the audience always delights in the sight of the ethereal angels as they "float" across the stage. The floating effect is created when the dancers take tiny-and-quick shuffling steps on* pointe, *producing the otherworldly illusion. Inspired by the Nutcracker angels, this angelic ornament, made of white-satin ribbon, metallic stars, and gold glitter, will look heavenly "dancing" across your Christmas tree.*

making "nutcracker angel"

1 Working on a protected surface, carefully shorten the length of the skewer to 4¼ in. (10.8cm) using the utility knife. Apply a dab of glue to one end of the skewer, and insert it into the hole in one bead. Repeat to glue a bead to the opposite end of the dowel.

2 Apply a coat of flesh-colored paint to one bead and a ½-in. (1.2cm) section of the skewer using the paint-brush. Let the paint dry. Add hair and facial features (the eyes, nose, and mouth) to the painted bead using the other paint colors; set the section aside.

3 Use a copier to size and print the patterns on pages 154 and 155 onto copy paper; then cut them out just outside the marked lines. Use your coin as a template for the halo, laying it on a piece of cardstock and tracing around it. Lay the "Wings" pattern on the cardstock, and trace around it. Use scissors to cut out the pattern pieces along the marked line.

4 Lay the wing and halo pieces on a protected work surface. Apply a thin coat of glue to one side and the edges of each piece. Pour a layer of glitter on the glue; allow the glue to dry. Tap off the excess glitter, and repeat to apply glitter to the other side of each piece.

Cut out the pattern pieces for the angel's skirt, bodice, and two sleeves. Lay each pattern piece on the white satin ribbon. Lift up each piece in turn, and apply a dab of glue and then a straight pin to secure the pattern pieces to the ribbon. Let the glue dry. Cut out the satin-and-paper pieces just outside the marked lines.

Lay the pattern pieces on a scrap of paper. Apply a thin bead of glue to the V-shaped sides of each sleeve section. Position and press a length of gold trim to the line of glue. Glue on a random array of gold stars to the skirt. Apply a thin bead of glue to the curved bottom of the skirt section. Position and press a length of gold trim to the line of glue; let the glue dry.

Measure and cut a 3-in.-by-2½-in. (7.6cm x 6.3cm) rectangle of batting, and wrap it around the skewer as shown, gluing the overlap to secure it. Wrap the batting using the satin rectangle, gluing the overlap to secure it.

Shape the satin-paper skirt section into a cone, gluing the overlap to secure it. Shape one sleeve into an elongated cone, gluing the overlap to secure it. Position and glue the sleeve to the body as shown, using a straight pin if necessary to secure the joint. Repeat to shape and glue the second sleeve.

Position and glue the wings and the halo to the back of the angel as shown.

Position and glue a 1-in. (2.5cm) length of gold trim around the angel's face. Let the glue dry.

"Nutcracker Angel" Patterns (shown at 90%; enlarge to 110%.)

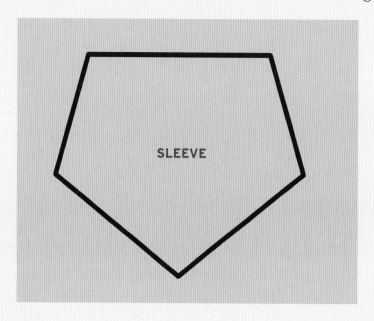

SLEEVE

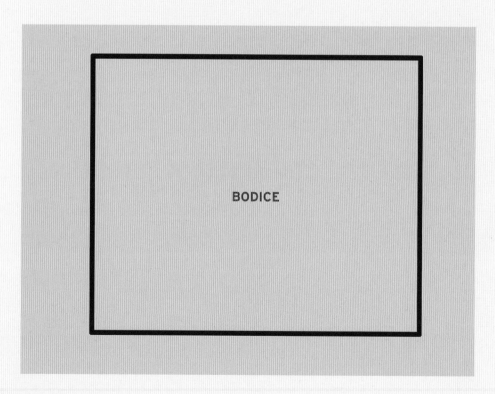

BODICE

WINGS

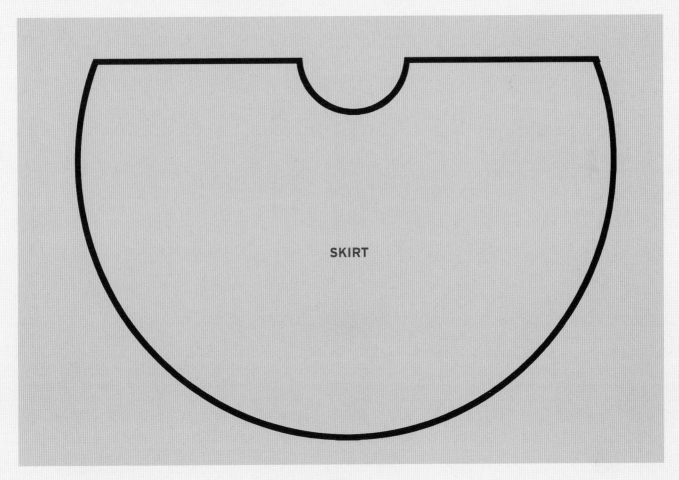

SKIRT

Swan Lake, Odette and the Corps de Ballet

Attending the Ballet

Anna Pavlova's passion for ballet was kindled from the moment she first gazed upon a magical production of *Sleeping Beauty* at the Mariinsky Theatre in St. Petersburg, Russia. Countless young dancers have been thus inspired by the experience of attending a professional ballet; the thrill of sitting in a darkened theatre, watching in awe as a real ballet unfolds upon the stage. It's a captivating experience, a moment of feverish inspiration when the audience is drawn inextricably into the rich tapestry of the story that the dancers create. Some of the most famous and popular ballets have become revered classics and are regularly performed, enchanting audiences throughout the world. ✛

"The ballet. I saw in the fugitive beauty of a dancer's gesture a symbol of life."

W. SOMERSET MAUGHAM

Swan Lake, Pas de Deux

illustrated ballet stories

SWAN LAKE, 1895

Choreographed by Marius Petipa and Lev Ivanov
Music by Peter Ilyich Tchiakovsky

At dusk, young Prince Siegfried comes across a beautiful swan that magically transforms before his eyes into the lovely Swan Queen, Odette. She tells him that the evil sorcerer, von Rothbart, has cast this terrible spell, which can only be broken by a pure declaration of love. Siegfried swears his love, drawing the wrath of Von Rothbart. Siegfried is then bewitched into thinking the black swan Odile—von Rothbart's daughter—is Odette, and swears his love to her, thus condemning Odette to be a swan forever. Rather than endure this fate, Odette throws herself into the lake, followed by a grief-stricken Siegfried. As morning approaches, the lovers' souls appear in the rising sun, united forever in eternity.

THE SLEEPING BEAUTY, 1890

Choreographed by Marius Petipa, Music by Peter Ilyich Tchiakovsky

Adapted from the famous fairytale, this is the story of the beautiful Princess Aurora. Due to the spell placed

upon her at birth by the wicked fairy Carabosse, Aurora pricks her finger on an enchanted spindle. Instead of dying, the Lilac Fairy's counter-spell simply puts Aurora to sleep. She and her court are awoken after 100 years by the kiss of the handsome Prince Florimund, who falls in love with Aurora instantly. They marry in a grand wedding celebration, attended by various other fairytale characters, such as Puss in Boots and Little Red Riding Hood.

COPPÉLIA, 1870

Choreographed by Arthur Saint-Léon, Music by Léo Delibes

Swanhilda finds her fiancé, Franz, flirting with Coppélia. Curious about this girl, she sneaks into the unsociable Dr. Coppélius' toyshop, where Coppélia lives, only to discover that the girl is in fact a mechanical doll. As Swanhilda hides in the shop, both Franz and Dr. Coppélius enter. The doctor intends to steal Franz's soul to instill in Coppélia. Swanhilda reveals herself, dressed as Coppélia, and convinces the doctor that he has brought Coppélia to life. Swanhilda reveals her identity, and she and Franz escape. The ballet ends with their marriage.

The Sleeping Beauty, The Lilac Fairy

GISELLE, 1841

Choreography by Jules Perrot
Music by Adolphe Adam

Count Albrecht, captivated by the young Giselle, disguises himself as a peasant to court her. Hilarion, who is also in love with Giselle, is filled with jealousy and reveals to Giselle Albrecht's true identity and his betrothal to the prince's daughter Bathilde. Giselle goes mad, dies of a broken heart, and joins the Wilis, a group of jilted maidens who die before their wedding night. When Albrecht is to die at the hands of the vengeful Wilis, Giselle's love saves his life.

ROMEO AND JULIET, 1965

Choreographed by Sir Kenneth
MacMillan
Music by Sergei Prokofiev

Based on Shakespeare's famous play, *Romeo and Juliet* depicts the story of two tragic lovers from the warring families of Montague and Capulet. Romeo declares his love to Juliet in the famous balcony scene. The two are secretly married, but then a misunderstanding leads Romeo to believe that Juliet is dead. Thus, he kills himself. Juliet, on discovering his death, stabs herself with Romeo's dagger. The Montagues and Capulets are left to lament over the deaths of Romeo and Juliet, and reunite in peace in the wake of the tragedy.

LES SYLPHIDES

(CHOPINIANA), 1909

Choreographed by Mikhail Fokine
Music by Frederic Chopin

Les Sylphides is a ballet that idealizes the Romantic period with a simple theme. Thus, it is considered the first abstract ballet. Set in a moonlit forest, it features a young poetic dreamer searching for beauty among the gathering of sylphs— wispy, fairy-like creatures clad in flowing white. Created with the composer in mind, the corps de ballet of sylphs is meant to personify the beautiful poetry of Chopin's nocturnes. The ballet was originally called Chopiniana, and is still known by that name in Russia.

PETRUSHKA, 1911

Choreographed by Mikhail Fokine,
Music by Igor Stravinsky

At a Russian fairground, three puppets are presented to a crowd by a Showman: the pretty Ballerina, the overconfident Moor, and the shy Petrushka. At night, the real-life drama of the puppets comes to life, with Petrushka fighting hopelessly against the Moor for the Ballerina's love. The Moor kills Petrushka, but the Showman assures the shocked crowd that it's only pretend. Suddenly, Petrushka's ghostly figure rises above the booth, mocking the Showman in revenge, freed from his power.

THE NUTCRACKER

Choreographed by Marius Petipa,
Lev Ivanov, and George Balanchine
Music by Peter Ilyich Tchiakovsky
1892 (Petipa and Ivanov);
1954 (Balanchine)

This ballet originated in Russia and has since become a Christmas classic throughout the world. At a Christmas party, Clara is heartbroken when her jealous brother, Fritz, breaks her Nutcracker doll. Her godfather Drosselmeyer fixes the toy and Clara watches as the Nutcracker comes to life to battle the Army of Mice. The Nutcracker then magically turns into a handsome prince and leads her to the Land of Sweets, where the Sugar Plum Fairy commands the sweets to dance for Clara and her Prince. After the dancing, Clara and her Prince are carried home by a magic sleigh.

A Dancer's Journal

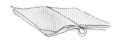 # notes from ballet class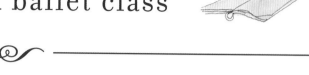

TEACHER

....

COMPLIMENTS / CORRECTIONS

....
....
....

TEACHER

....
....

COMPLIMENTS / CORRECTIONS

....
....
....

TEACHER

....
....

COMPLIMENTS / CORRECTIONS

....
....
....

FAVORITE TEACHERS

....
....
....

THINGS THAT I WANT TO WORK ON

....
....
....

DANCERS WHO INSPIRE ME

....
....
....

QUALITIES THAT I WOULD LIKE
TO EMULATE

....
....
....

memories from summer programs

FRIENDS WHO I MET

COMPETITIONS THAT I HAVE ENTERED

UNIQUE EXPERIENCES THAT I HAD

COMPETITIONS THAT I WOULD LIKE TO ENTER

PERFORMANCES IN WHICH I DANCED

MY DANCE CAREER GOALS

special memories of my performances

PRODUCTION

PRODUCTION

PRODUCTION

DATE

DATE

DATE

ROLE(S) PERFORMED

ROLE(S) PERFORMED

ROLE(S) PERFORMED

PHOTO

PHOTO

PHOTO

ROLES THAT I WOULD LIKE TO DANCE IN THE FUTURE

some of my favorites

MUSIC

COSTUME(S)

BALLET(S)

BALLET COMPANIES

BALLET VARIATION(S)

BALLET BOOK(S)

CHOREOGRAPHER(S)

BALLET CD(S) AND DVD(S)

 creating my own ballet

STORY

TYPE OF MUSIC

CAST OF CHARACTERS

COSTUME DESIGNS

SCENERY

CHOREOGRAPHY

[Sketches]

designing my own ballet crafts

BALLET CRAFTS THAT I WANT TO MAKE

SOURCES AND RESOURCES

+++

SOURCES

B & J Fabrics
525 7th Ave., 2nd Fl.
New York, NY 10019
212-354-8150
www.bandjfabrics.com

Dancer's Depot
870 High Ridge Rd.
Stamford, CT 06905
203-609-9009

Good, Goods
859 Post Rd.
Darien, CT 06820
203-655-8100

Knotty Girl Knit & Yarn Club
119 Post Rd.
Fairfield, CT 06824
203-254-KNIT
www.Knottygirlknits.com

Koenig Art Emporium
153 E. Main St.
Mount Kisco, NY 10549
914-666-6949
www.koenigartemporium.com

M & J Trimming
1008 6th Ave. at 38th St.
New York, NY 10018
800-965-8746
www.mjtrim.com

Metropolitan Impex, Inc.
966 Ave. of the America's
New York, NY 10018
212-502-5243
www.metropolitanimpex.com

Rima Day Custom Tutus
Dance Costumer
203-253-1294
rimaday@mac.com

Rogers & Goffigon
D & D Building
979 3rd Ave.
New York, NY 10022
212-888-3242

Toho Shoji (New York) Inc.
990 Sixth Ave.
New York, NY 10018
212-868-7465

RESOURCES
(See Web sites for store locations where applicable.)

American Eagle Outfitters
888-232-4535
www.ae.com

Beadworks
877-405-6107
www.beadworks.com

Body Wrappers
800-323-0786
www.bodywrappers.com

Capezio East
800-533-1887
www.capeziodance.net

Discount Dance Supply
800-328-7107
www.discountdance.com

Duralee Fabrics
800-275-3872
www.duralee.com

Joyce Trimming, Inc.
800-719-7133
www.ejoyce.com

Michaels: The Arts and Crafts Store
800-642-4235
www.michaels.com

Papyrus
800-789-1649
www.papyrusonline.com

The Rag Shop
973-423-1303
www.ragshop.com

Tutu.com
877-888-8266
www.tutu.com

Rosalie O'Connor Photography
212-866-7597
www.rosalieoconnor.com

Haskin Illustrations
Fine line drawings and watercolors
christinaaleta11@hotmail.com

ACKNOWLEDGMENTS

Like creating a ballet, creating this book was a collaboration of many talented people, and I want to thank them for helping in the production of this work: Carol Endler Sterbenz, Senior Editor of Home Arts, for her courage, talent, and belief in this book; Rosalie O'Connor, principal photographer, for her beautiful photographs, and David Morris Cunningham, for his wonderful lighting; Steven Mays for the instructional photographs; Genevieve A. Sterbenz, producer of photography, for her steadfast dedication to getting things done; and Brett Raphael at *Connecticut Ballet*, and Cheryl Kemeny and Mariner Pezza of *The Crystal Theatre*. Special thanks to the talented designers: Dee Stanziano, Stina Ramos, Beth Vogl, Jeannie Finlay, Rima Day, Tina Dean, Olivia Just, Genevieve A. Sterbenz, and Lena Bunevitsky; and also to Patricia Czescik, and Mary Rhode for their sewing talent; and costumer Marie Velaquez. Thank you to Olivia Just, a wonderful daughter and talented dancer, for all her support and assistance; my sisters, Stephanie Haskin and Holley Egloff, and my brother, Ian Haskin, for their support and encouragement; my friend, Susan Feldmar, for her creative opinions and advice. A special thanks to Amy O'Neill Houck, technical editor, and to Kathryn Hammill, Diane Shaw, and Jennifer Blanco of Goodesign, for their beautiful book design.

Thank you, also, to all the talented dancers, teachers, and the pianist for being a part of this book.

Top Row: Hayley Verbeke, Henry Rosenberg, Riana Kami, Anika Tallis, (teacher) Jahain Bechtold, Paulina Waski, Caitlin McAndrew, Alison Goldsmith, William Rosenberg **Bottom Row:** Cassidy McAndrew, Lilly Gregory, Riley Robinson, Gabriella Zarlenga, and Margaret Epstein; Skyla Baron and Adrian Velaquez (not pictured).

Top Row: Elizabeth Bastias-Butler, Lydia Montagese, Ellany Abbot, Ulises Ordana, (teacher) Devani Maijala, Olivia Just, Claire Mazza, Anastasia Puglisi, and Lauren Kaye **Bottom Row:** Carolyn Geils, Christine Geils, Grace Shay, and Sandra Ross; Serena MacKool and (pianist) Allan Greene (not pictured).

KNIT AND CROCHET ABBREVIATIONS

bsc	beaded single crochet	rem	remaining
btr	beaded triple crochet	RS	right side
bc	beaded chain	sc	single crochet
BO	bind off	sl	slip
ch	chain	sl st	slip stitch
CN	cable needle	sm	slip marker
CO	cast on	ssk	slip 2 sts as if to knit, then knit
cl	double crochet cluster	st st	stockinette stitch
dc	double crochet	st(s)	stitch(es)
dcdec	double crochet decrease	tr	treble crochet
dec	decrease		
dpns	double pointed needles		
ea	each		
ext	Extended		
garter	knit every row		
hdc	half double crochet		
inc	increase		
k	knit		
k2tog	knit 2 stitches together		
lp(s)	loop(s)		
M1	make 1		
p	purl		
psso	pass slipped stich over		
p2tog	purl 2 stitches together		
pat	pattern		
pm	place marker		

INDEX